". . . *Systems of education should be adopted and pursued which may . . . implant in the minds of the American youth the principles of virtue and of liberty and inspire them with just and liberal ideas of government and with an inviolable attachment to their own country.*"

Noah Webster,
1780

"*The right to mold the political, moral and religious opinions of his children, is a right exclusively and jealously reserved by our own laws to every parent; and for the government to attempt . . . to stand in the parent's place, is an undertaking of very questionable policy.*"

Report of the Committee on Education,
Massachusetts House of Representatives, 1840

DISESTABLISHMENT A SECOND TIME

GENUINE PLURALISM FOR AMERICAN SCHOOLS

Rockne M. McCarthy
James W. Skillen
William A. Harper

CHRISTIAN
UNIVERSITY
PRESS

A SUBSIDIARY OF CHRISTIAN COLLEGE CONSORTIUM
AND WILLIAM B. EERDMANS PUBLISHING COMPANY
Grand Rapids, Michigan

Available from William B. Eerdmans Publishing Co.
255 Jefferson Ave. SE, Grand Rapids, Mich. 49503

Library of Congress Cataloging in Publication Data

McCarthy, Rockne.
Disestablishment a second time.

Includes bibliographical references.
1. Education—United States—History.   2. Pluralism.
I. Skillen, James W.   II. Harper, William A. (William
Arthur), 1939-   III. Title.
LA205.M48   1982   370'.973   82-9409
ISBN 0-8028-1931-1   AACR2

To
Joan, Mark, Kristin, and Maygann McCarthy
Doreen, Jeanene, and Jamie Skillen
Lillian and Colin Harper

Who have been our most loving and valued
supporters in this communal project

CONTENTS

FOREWORD

THE authors of this book have been waiting in the wings for several years. Now they are on stage. When I met them about five years ago, they confronted me with arguments and a manuscript. While I had and have a basic disagreement on a central point, I found in their treatment a fresh reading of early American history and a compelling plea for change in the present. The scholarship was sound, the writing clear and cogent, the advocacy exciting. The book looked like a natural. Whoever does not like the book will have to think of me as an unindicted coconspirator, because I confess that from the first encounter I made efforts to see it published.

Publishers concurred in these positive judgments of the manuscript. They held back for one reason. As they read the mood and curiosities of the American people, the times were not ripe for such a book. It was not relevant.

Yet, just a few years later few will question the book's relevance to the moods and curiosities of the citizenry. A new civil argument, usually carried on very uncivilly, has broken out concerning the character of American common life. Concern over morals and values, much of it grounded in religion, occupies the minds of Americans only less than their concern over the economy and foreign policy, if we are to believe the evidence of the polls. The religious community has divided between a belligerent radical right and a disorganized and ill-focused set of moderate forces. Long passive conservative religionists who have previously kept their distance from politics have plunged into the thick of the fray, breaking all the rules of the game that they had set up and observed only a few short years before. Why? Because of the urgency of the American moral situation, they will argue.

What churches do about the moral condition is their business. But there is one set of institutions that is everyone's business: the public schools. Somehow whenever the issue of the American character and its values heats up, the conflict focuses on these schools. A nation that lacks a tax-supported established church almost instinctively transfers some expectations of a quasi-religious character to this "junior established church of the American public religion." Particularly because of the decisiveness of elementary and secondary education in the shaping of people, adults find it natural to put great pressure on the schools. If homes, neighborhoods, voluntary associations, or churches are in trouble or even collapse, the public schools are supposed to survive to compensate.

During these years it has become clear that the schools cannot support all the weight the society places on them. They overpromised in their boom years, when they overbuilt. Now with declining birth rates many of their classrooms are empty, and the public, having grown mistrustful and having been victimized by inflation, is suspicious of the claims of education. Voting with their pocketbooks, citizens in many communities have inhibited experiment and expansion. The fiscal crisis, however, is only a symptom of the root problem. Withholding tax support has not been as drastic an act as withholding consent from the public venture, or withholding assent from the faith it seems to take to keep a complex institution prosperous.

The schools are not alone. Economist Kenneth Boulding and others have isolated a "crisis of legitimacy" that has afflicted most institutions including government, politics, the military, higher education, and the churches. But the public schools are more vulnerable than most other institutions, and they have not been able to weather all the tests. In 1980 as a member of the President's Commission for a National Agenda for the Eighties, I was among fifty citizens who probed the health of American agencies. I would come home from many inquiries, panels, or site visitations with a glimmer of hope for the economy, the defense community, and the like. But seldom, whether in Austin, Los Angeles, Washington, or Chicago, did we hear clarity of direction from or hope for educators.

The public gloom may be too deep, and citizens may be making scapegoats out of the convenient public schools. One can in fact point to much about the schools that is healthy. They are likely to survive in some form or other, chastened by their recent experiences. During this period of striking out against them, citizens have invented fictitious pasts, Good Old Days that never existed, and asked the schools to live up to them. But after reconstruction the schools are not soon likely to assume the assured place they held before. During this period of their crisis it is only natural for thoughtful citizens to engage in basic questioning about the models of education which the United States has adopted. What Americans take for granted as the only way to see a pluralistic society prosper is not a pattern borrowed from or precisely duplicated anywhere else — not even so near as Canada.

The authors of this book show some regard for the past achievements of the public schools and are not out to kill them, only to supplement them. I have to confess more uneasiness than they over the plight of these schools and over the prospect of an America so chopped up into sects, ethnic groups, economic classes, and interest groups that it would lose one of its few surviving public forums. Take away all the romance that nostalgic people have associated with schools and they still show impressive achievements. Limited as they were, they did help millions in many generations come out of isolation into the public arena where they were to spend their lives. Though the schools did have covert ideologies, and sometimes quite overt ones, they also provided a neutral ground between tribes that otherwise would not have tolerated one another. So I shall continue to care about and worry over public schools more than these authors do. But the disposition of the existing public schools is not the chief item on their agenda. They are interested not in replacing but in complementing such schools.

Our writers do not have to invent alternatives. America already has great networks of private institutions. Sensing the anti-Catholic ethos of the nineteenth-century public schools, Roman Catholics set up their own system, and, despite some traumas after Vatican II, the Catholic schools are one surviving model. Missouri Synod Lutherans, Seventh-Day Adventists, the Christian Reformed, Quakers, and Episcopalians all established Christian day schools. Private schools, including university laboratory schools, have been accessible to upper middle class and wealthy families whose support of public education has often been of the lip service variety. Militant rightists, who have agitated most vehemently against "atheistic" or "secular humanistic" public education, have been opening new Protestant schools with regularity in recent years. These models are a diverse lot, offering everything from abjectly primitive education to tony prep school elitism, from benign Christian faith to ideology a bit short of savagery. Many parents are seeking them out today, but finding it hard to support their devotion financially. The authors of this book have in mind making the lives of such parents easier by suggesting that the current patterns of support are not fixed in concrete or the

Constitution. They would like to see more experiment in funding education. We shall let them state that case, which they do with more eloquence than I could bring to the cause.

I was called in as a witness on the historical issue, which makes up the bulk of this book. These scholars have reread the history of American education, and, if we give them a chance, they may help make history by smoking out better than most others a certain question of American public ethos and ideology. Their curiosities lead them back to the Founding Fathers, most notably to Jefferson. To many of his contemporaries he was what fundamentalists today would call a "secular humanist." Insofar as he helped charter American public education, then, Jefferson could be seen as a secularizer.

He was anything but that. The third president had a very clear para-Christian vision. It was informed by respect for the man Jesus of Nazareth, illumined by a scholarly study of the Bible few lay people in American history have matched, and centered in a concept of Reason and Order in a universe of meaning. Jefferson and those in his lineage have been very critical of the churches, whose faith they saw as particular, sectarian, cramping, and self-serving. The public faith, on the other hand, was supposed to be universal, accessible to all, simply the "truth about life" to all reasonable people. Our authors, however, show that Jeffersonianism or the milder Franklinianism, for example, was a sect among the sects, a faith among the faiths. It was privileged because it had helped bring about American religious freedom while the other sects squabbled. Since it was voiced by Enlightened statesmen it became informally established. Inevitably some of its vision entered the schools.

Most Americans, however, did not accept the public faith as their saving faith. They stayed with the churches, and through many nineteenth-century revivals chose against Jeffersonianism and for evangelicalisms and catholicisms again and again. Still, the Enlightenment faith helped connect the strands of public education, primarily because of the way the Protestants used public authority to establish the common schools. In the middle of the nineteenth century the public schools were organized as extensions of the Protestant empire. The schools were quite consistently anti-Catholic. They carefully graded ethnic groups and races, with the old-stock Protestants being at the core, and Catholic, Jewish, Eastern Orthodox, to say nothing of African, Asian, and Native American, peoples and religions relegated to an inferior status. The public school system we know today was, at its inception, not the junior wing of a Jeffersonian church, but the tax-supported wing of the evangelical churches.

More than this book recognizes, it is the simple "pluralization" of America, challenging the old Protestant hegemony, that has led to much of the current attack on public education. The New Protestant Right might simply be the most recent, maybe the last, of the ethnic groups or interest groups that have arisen in the past generation. School texts have been changed to reflect the values of blacks, Hispanics, Orientals, Jews, women, homosexuals—everyone but the old-stock Protestants, particularly those from lower income groups or Bible Belt backgrounds. Now, full of resentment and seeking revenge, such Protestants have exercised the "privilege of historical backwardness" and, armed with the latest technology—television, direct mail, sophisticated political organizational techniques—have made their sudden move. School boards and library boards have already felt the point of their attack.

Fighting against "secular humanism," they are really fighting for the restoration of the Protestant empire's values as the central norms in public education. Their "scientific creationism" as an alternative to evolutionary theory in science is disguised as science itself. But the whole motive for presenting it is creedal; the key hermeneutical jumping off place is a particular text in Genesis, and other believers in the Bible, be they Catholics, Jews, or moderate Protestants, recognize it as such. The New Protestant Right "goes for broke." It explicitly wants an establishment—they call it a reestablishment—of public schools that perpetuate the evangelical Protestant outlook. Failing that, they will set up their own schools.

This book, I am happy to say, does not try to win back in the ethos what it cannot win through the Constitution. It is not out to exploit the majority status of American Protestantism by establishing Protestant or even generalized Christian faith in public schools and making second class citizens of all who do not share that faith. The authors have no such belligerence in mind. They are in this sense more modest, as they argue for the possibilities of a genuine pluralism. They want the interests of many more kinds of parents protected in the future. This effort is plausible and merits applause even from those who may not agree with their specific proposals.

This Foreword has implied some minor disagreements. It is not a "blurb" by a fawning admirer. Since the three authors agree with each other, the writer of the Foreword should not be expected to make all votes unanimous. Therefore it is in order to advance the argument of the book by raising the point that makes me most uneasy. The Jeffersonian argument and the case for pluralistic models are the strengths of the book. But these claims also give the impression that schools are and have to be more religious than in fact they have been or really must be.

Americans today have accepted anthropological definitions of religion that are so broad they exclude nothing. Faith, once seen as Protestant, then Christian, then Judaeo-Christian, then theistic, is now extended to include all worldviews, outlooks, notions, concerns, and glimmerings. Now it may well be true that, pushed to the extreme, all of these are grounded somehow in a sense of the sacred. But religion includes more than the cognitive. There must be fairly elaborate patterns of socialization, myth, metaphysics, behavioral consequence, symbol, rite, ceremony, and story in order to give definable form to a religion. Admittedly, the public schools have elements of these, but they are not often sufficiently coherent or coercive that they are a threat to other particular faiths.

I agree with John Courtney Murray that in serious debate citizens have to "go up higher" into the realms of metaphysics, ethics, or theology. I agree also that Americans are not likely to agree very much on any of these subjects. Not all "going up higher" has to result in arriving at something like either the Jeffersonian disguised Deistic faith or the Protestant establishment's biblical imposition. The Supreme Court is not merely not opposed to discussing religious and theological themes in the schools; it has in fact encouraged such discussion. The schools cannot be turned into churches. They cannot be used for evangelizing, for proselytizing. So the Court has to fumble for terms like teaching "about" religion. We all know that religious assumptions do lie behind such attempts. But we are not talking about a pure realm beyond history. We are talking about a pluralistic society where people have to act with restraint and respect for each other. So Enlightenment, secular, Jewish, Christian, and "world religious" themes do belong in public education. The Enlightenment version, our authors say, should not be privileged. Agreed. But are all the uses of reason, inquiry, examination, historical study, and studies in the humanities and social sciences as religious in the first place as they imply?

While the authors argue for alternatives to public schools, then, I would also argue that we have too readily begun to regard the schools not as *insufficiently* religious but as *too* religious. It is time to cool the temperature, to lower the voice. People can discuss Plato and Aristotle, Renaissance humanism, Kant's categorical imperative and Mills's utilitarianism, loyalty and patriotism and ideals and principles without always at all points "going up higher" into theology and to articulated religious systems. Until and unless we can restore some of that more neutral sense to public education we will find that the public forum as such will disappear completely. America will be left with self-enclosed, solipsistic, mutually exclusive tribes. We shall be condemned to interpret our texts in isolation, to move in our own hermeneutical circles, to keep our tribes out of touch with all others.

That approach has been tried and is being tried all over the world, from the New Guinea bush to Africa to Lebanon. The name for it is not pluralism or dialogue or civil disagreement but tribal warfare. Civil argument, political debate, confrontation of traditions, all these are going to have to occur somewhere, with or without alternative school systems. When such argument is not given a forum, the consequences are too serious to consider with equanimity. They can best be avoided if we are less insistent that all alternatives to our own religion are themselves aggressive and belligerent religions, subversive of our own.

MARTIN E. MARTY

The University of Chicago

PREFACE

QUESTIONS about the relationship between the state and schools have engaged scholars and public officials for centuries. In contemporary democratic countries, the same questions often are asked by groups of citizens who first become concerned when they observe declining quality in their children's education or when they sense a lack of justice in public policies that affect education. It is important that scholars and public officials keep in close touch with the motivations, concerns, and wisdom of citizens who experience the effects of public policies, who are continually in touch with the schools where they or their children spend hours each day.

The present volume is the outgrowth of a sustained dialogue between the authors and one group of concerned citizens. The authors, who enjoyed a fruitful and enjoyable collaboration on this project for more than three years, first met each other through the Association for Public Justice, a Christian citizen's movement attempting to address both policy and structural issues in the public arena. Grants from the Association and from the APJ Education Fund brought the authors together for three successive summers of common reading, discussion, and writing. Apart from the Association for Public Justice (including its vision, purpose, and financial support) this book could not have been written.

As the writing of the book progressed we became increasingly conscious of the great value of scholarly cooperation. Much can be learned, self-criticism is facilitated, a community of thought can be developed, and patient endurance is strengthened — all through participation in a common project. We are grateful to the Association for Public Justice for making our work possible. And we are thankful for all the help that we received from numerous friends and readers. Donald E. King, Jr., deserves a special word of thanks for having done so much research, typing, and organizational work on our behalf. A number of persons read the final draft and contributed many valuable suggestions and comments. Among these were Peter DeBoer, Mark Noll, Henry Vander Goot, Walfred Peterson, and Daniel McGarry. None of these persons can be held accountable for the final product, but we thank them for their very great help.

We are especially grateful to Martin E. Marty who not only read the typescript but also agreed to write the Foreword. While giving us considerable encouragement, he has also raised some important questions, and we offer his Foreword as the first step toward the dialogue that we want to carry forward with others on this important subject.

ROCKNE M. MCCARTHY
JAMES W. SKILLEN
WILLIAM A. HARPER

DISESTABLISHMENT
A SECOND TIME

INTRODUCTION

EDUCATION is one of the chief concerns and expenses of the American republic, but the nation has never reached complete agreement about what the government's proper responsibility should be for education. Is it the proper task of government to establish schools or should it restrict itself to the indirect aid and encouragement of education? Should the primary responsibility for education reside with parents, local communities, states, or the federal government? If education is entrusted to the responsibility of local communities, what is the proper role of parents and state and federal governments in education? Should "public" schools alone receive the financial support of the government, or should "private" schools also receive public funds? Is it legitimate for the agencies of government to control and adjust the structures and populations of the schools for the purpose of opposing racial segregation or some other social ill, or should the schools be free from such "noneducational" interference?

Educators, scholars, political leaders, parents, lawyers, church leaders, and Supreme Court Justices continue to ask these questions and debate the issues involved. The importance of education is seldom questioned, but the task of government and the responsibility of the public for education remains much in dispute.

The purpose of this book is to examine critically the place and function of schools in the American republic and to suggest some structural changes that could lead to greater justice in this area. Our primary concern is not so much with the curricula and organization within the schools, but rather with the public legal relationship between education and the state. We want to ask about the relative justice and injustice of the laws that have come to structure education in the United States.

In order to accomplish this purpose we will explore the subject using several approaches. We will make use of historical,

1

philosophical, sociological, legal, economic, and comparative political studies. We are not offering another history of education or of constitutional law, nor will we take up all the contemporary plaudits and criticisms of education in America. Rather we will try to interpret the problems, ambiguities, and dilemmas inherent in the way education and the state are related in this country in order to point to a framework which can lead to greater justice.

Two decades ago Bernard Bailyn challenged historians and other scholars to broaden the study of education by viewing it "not only as formal pedagogy but as the entire process by which a culture transmits itself across the generations."[1] To study education, said Bailyn, means to study its "intricate involvements with the rest of society" and to uncover those critical historical junctures where the elements of "our familiar present" begin to emerge from a somewhat "unfamiliar past."[2] The present system of American education has not existed from eternity. It came into being through a process of historical struggle and decision making. Taking up Bailyn's challenge, we want to ask, "Why, when, and how did we Americans decide upon the present public legal structure of education? Could we have chosen another course or other options? If so, why did we not do so?"

In recent years dozens of scholars representing different perspectives and motivated by different purposes have taken up Bailyn's challenge to reexamine critically the field of American education. Michael B. Katz's *Class, Bureaucracy, and Schools*, first published in 1971, is now considered by many a classic of modern historical/sociological analysis.[3] Libertarian critics of the American political system, such as William F. Rickenbacker, Murray N. Rothbard, and E. G. West, have taken careful aim at education in order to make their case for more individual freedom and less government.[4] The Marxist critics of American capitalism, Samuel Bowles and Herbert Gintis, studied the history of educational "reform" in the United States in order to prove that political, legal, and educational changes are the products of the deeper contradictions of economic life.[5] The list of authors and viewpoints could be extended.

In what follows we will try to be attentive to the insights and criticisms coming from many different sources. At the same time, however, our intention is to do more than merely debate with and borrow from those who have already made their case. We are convinced that there are matters which have not yet been discussed, a perspective which has not yet been opened up, insights that have not yet been offered. In particular we are interested in the way that American political and educational institutions have been defined and determined by the civil-religious dynamic that has operated at the root of modern democratic nation building. The historical realities of legal, constitutional, social, and economic change cannot be overlooked or belittled. Nevertheless, certain characteristics of the American political system and the public school system cannot be grasped in economic, sociological, or legal terms alone. We hope to offer a fuller understanding of the link between state and school in this country.

In Chapter One we will present in brief compass our thesis about the relationship between modern civil religion on the one hand and the political and educational institutions that were established in early America on the other. Chapters Two and Three will examine the republican philosophy of Thomas Jefferson and others who created the essential political framework for the development of a public school system such as that which evolved in America. Chapter Four will test the arguments of the preceding chapters by showing how and why the modern public school system was formally organized in the middle of the nineteenth century.

The triadic relationship among politics, education, and religion finally came to the attention of the Supreme Court in the twentieth century. In Chapters Five and Six our critical examination of the Court's responses to some of the constitutional dilemmas inherent in this complex relationship will demonstrate that the Court's predicament can only be grasped adequately from the perspective that we will have elucidated in previous chapters.

The last two chapters carry us beyond the present problems to possible solutions and alternatives. We look first, in Chapter Seven, at the political and educational systems in some other democratic countries where different assumptions and convictions have been at work in the process of establishing systems of public education. In conclusion we present our own suggestions for the kind of structural change in the public legal order of the United States that will lead to greater justice for schools.

CHAPTER 1

CIVIL RELIGION AND THE FOUNDATIONS OF THE REPUBLIC

THE nature of "civil religion" has been much discussed and debated in recent years.[1] For the purposes of this book we will consider civil religion from the point of view of the structure of the state and the responsibility of government rather than from the position of the religiously responsive individual or community. From the viewpoint of the political structure, a civil religion is the public legal establishment of a religiously rooted world and life view. Since modern states are made up of individuals, groups, and institutions of different basic commitments, the political establishment of one religion inevitably restricts the civil rights of those individuals, groups, and institutions that do not hold the established view, thus excluding them from full participation in the public legal community.

Given our understanding of civil religion, the questions with which we will be concerned in the following chapters include the following: Is a state free of religious impositions upon its citizens simply by virtue of the fact that it has no established church? Can a state avoid altogether the imposition of "beliefs" upon its citizens? Can it maintain a neutral distance from all religious matters? If a state remains free of entanglement with churches, synagogues, and other similar institutions, does it still run the danger of entanglement with religion by other means and through other kinds of institutions? How do schools fit into the picture framed by the First Amendment's stipulations regarding the relationship between government and religion?

While it is certainly true that major economic and social changes accompanied the formation of modern states, so did profound religious change. Indeed, the political struggles over religion were so basic and serious that they frequently outweighed social and economic issues in the minds of the factions that were attempting to create and control the new states. Moreover, while a twentieth-century American may have the impression that our country's political-religious struggles were all settled long ago, it is our contention that American federal and state constitutions have framed a civil-religious structure that perpetuates such struggles with respect to politics, religion, and education.

Apart from any questions concerning the personal piety and religious habits of individuals in the United States, the very political structure of the republic poses unsettled problems and dilemmas for contemporary America. In order to demonstrate this point we must begin with a brief exploration of some European roots of the American colonial experience.

THE HIGH MIDDLE AGES

In what we now call the High Middle Ages of European civilization the church was more than a private association with limited ceremonial and educational functions. As one of the few differentiated institutions of medieval society it actually served as the chief integrator of cultural life. Joseph R. Strayer points out that economic life, Gothic art, chivalric poetry, scholastic philosophy, and the university system of education were all part of an organic, integrated, homogeneous culture.[2] The civilization of the twelfth century, he says, "was remarkably self-sufficient and self-consistent; it had a flavor, a texture, almost a personality, of its own."[3] The integral identity of this culture was due in large part to the shaping power of the Roman Catholic Church, a church which also functioned as the primary force in what we now call the state or the political community.

Strayer's comment about scholastic philosophy and the university system as central to the social structure of the High Middle Ages points to the role that education plays in promoting societal cohesion, identity, and unity. Education in both its formal and informal expressions is one of the means by which groups share together, defend, and propagate their deepest convictions about the meaning of life. In a rural, homogeneous community the family and extended kinships may be largely responsible for transferring these convictions and perspectives. In that situation it is often impossible to discover where the family leaves off and the larger community begins; education, transferring the wisdom and values of the community as a whole, remains within the family. In differentiated societies, however, formal education becomes more independent, so that the process of instructing the community as a whole is increasingly vested in schools and universities rather than in the family.

In the European High Middle Ages the importance of formal institutions of education for maintaining the integral unity of Christendom was well understood. In the cathedral and parish churches, guild schools, monasteries, and universities, the aim was to provide instruction within the framework of the assumptions and values of a Christian society. The medieval triad of *regnum, sacerdotium,* and *studium* expressed well the ideal of one commonwealth, one church, and a common academic study of the moral and natural law which undergirded the unity of culture and faith.[4]

Although medieval writers distinguished *regnum* (political authority) and *sacerdotium* (religious authority), the state and the church could not be divided. Medieval theory insisted there was only one society, the church, under one king, Christ. And although medieval writers distinguished between *studium* (education) and *sacerdotium*, students in medieval schools were in one sense all clergy, and the curriculum was essentially clerical.[5] In the Middle Ages the liberal arts, the *trivium* and the *quadrivium*, were pursued in the interest of the church, for the whole society, to the glory of God.

RENAISSANCE AND REFORMATION

The Renaissance and Protestant Reformation challenged and then broke the organic unity of the medieval world. The "conflict of spirits" that emerged was not confined to pamphlets nor contained within ecclesiastical and university debates. The question of political power could not be avoided. When the bloodletting of the Thirty Years War ended in 1648 with the Peace of Westphalia, Europe was clearly divided religiously and politically with the consequence that each major confessional group was granted its own territorial arena within which it could become or remain dominant. Lutheranism took over much of Germany and the Scandinavian countries; Anglicanism eventually came out on top in England; Calvinism came to rule in Geneva, Scotland, and the Netherlands; Catholicism retained its hold in much of Central Europe and in Spain; and civic humanism grew to preeminence in certain Italian city-states. In all these different religiously and politically defined territories it was still assumed that education could not be a matter of indifference but should be carefully directed by the public authorities as a means of propagating and enforcing a particular way of life among a people.

The recovery of classical antiquity during the Renaissance meant that the ancient Greek view of education came to new life. Education was one of the special concerns of the Greek city-state or *polis*. Though the law appears to have been less rigorous in Athens than in Sparta, where the father could have nothing to do with the formal education of his son, Athenian children were, nevertheless, instructed by masters appointed by the political authorities. Plato made quite clear the motive for this: "Parents ought not to be free to send or not to send their children to the masters whom the city has chosen, for the children belong less to their parents than to the city."[6]

During the Renaissance many of the ideals of the ancient Greek polis reemerged to influence the Italian city-states. Guided by many of the same concerns that the ancient Greeks held, Renaissance scholars saw the need for public support of education. Vittorino da Feltre, considered by some the most important and successful schoolmaster of the Renaissance, argued that the state had a special interest in education. According to Vittorino, "The education of children is a matter of more than private interest; it concerns the State, which indeed regards the right training of the young as, in certain aspects, within its proper sphere."[7] Although not all scholars agreed with Vittorino, it was clear that during this period nonecclesiastical control and support of education were on the increase.[8] Renaissance scholars and princes no less than the Greeks or medieval clerics recognized the importance of education in defining and holding together a people.

The leaders of the Protestant Reformation also recognized the important role education plays as a means of social integration. In Germany, for example, the Reformation undercut the power of the Catholic Church and swept away the existing ecclesiastical controls over the schools. To meet this new situation Martin Luther appealed to the temporal authorities, the mayors and councilmen of Germany, to increase their support for and control over education.[9] In the wake of the Lutheran Reformation the bitter conflict between the Catholic Church and the secular authorities over the control of education came to an end. City officials assumed full power over the schools, and princes established schools and universities throughout their principalities.[10]

Luther dealt with education in tracts and sermons and letters. His most important work on education, "Letter to the Mayors and Aldermen of all the Cities of Germany in Behalf of Christian Schools," was written in 1524.[11] The letter was the beginning of

Luther's efforts to place education under the control of the temporal authorities. In Luther's mind compulsory education was a necessary part of the church-state establishment. The state, church, and school were all to play a crucial role in the articulation and support of a Christian society.

John Calvin was able to realize his ideal for education more easily than Luther. While Luther had to deal with large numbers of separate states and independent cities, Calvin had the advantage of being able to focus his attention on a single city-state. At Geneva Calvin fashioned a community in which education played an extremely important role in defining the city as a whole.[12] Calvin's understanding of the relation of state, church, and school was to influence, among others, the New England Puritans.

The competing world views that were represented in the different political-religious territories of Reformation Europe ushered in and guided the development of new political structures — the modern states. For decades each confessional group clung to the established principle of religious uniformity enforced by the power of the sword. "One faith, one territory" continued to be the accepted pattern of sixteenth- and seventeenth-century life. Although the medieval ecclesiastical unity had broken down and a variety of confessional groups had emerged, the new political structure of any given area still did little to protect the civil rights of religiously dissenting individuals, groups, and institutions. Within each territory political authorities supported a civil-religious order which in turn defined the cultural unity of the people.

The only major challenge to this political tradition came from the Anabaptist groups that emerged in the course of the Reformation. Desiring freedom to be left alone to follow their own understanding of primitive Christianity, they formed voluntary associations and rejected the attempts of political authorities to enforce religious uniformity. Viewing all civil authority as outside the perfection of Christ, Anabaptist groups rejected any political participation. The various European political authorities judged such a position to be subversive of the political order, and the Anabaptists were threatened and persecuted from all sides.

The Anabaptists were a people without political power or influence; they controlled no state in which to establish and maintain their own schools. They did not look to compulsory political authority to guarantee instruction in their way of life. That they survived prolonged persecution is a testimony to the effectiveness of their ability to sustain and transmit within their group their unique values and perspective on life without political support. They were, however, an exception to the rule of a people using the power of the sword to enforce religious and educational uniformity.

EARLY AMERICAN FOUNDATIONS

The settlement of the "new world" took place at a time when people still believed that every territory commanded a common faith. Among other things, America provided an opportunity for different confessional groups to build social and political communities consistent with their world views. As Sidney Mead explains, the original intention of the colonists was to perpetuate the pattern of religious uniformity in the different settlements.[13] Thus the same civil-religious pattern exhibited in Europe was initially transplanted in the new world.

In the Puritan colonies of New England the faith of the "saints" guided their errand into the wilderness and provided the basis for the Bible commonwealth. In the Massachusetts Bay Colony the Puritans planted the seeds of a new civil-religious order. Even the Separatists at Plymouth put forth their beliefs as the basis of the public legal order of their colony.[14] In the South, and particularly in Virginia, the older Anglican religion was officially (if not fully in practice) established as the basis for the society which emerged under the first charter of Virginia in 1606 and the Royal Colony in 1624. Likewise, in the earliest settlements in the "middle colonies," from the Dutch Reformed settlements on the Hudson to the Swedish communities along the Delaware, an individual's political standing was based in part upon his or her acceptance of the orthodox religious beliefs of the community. In each of the original settlements dissenting individuals, groups, or institutions were excluded from full participation in the political community.

The European understanding of education as a means of social integration was also imported by the first settlers that came to America.[15] In each settlement the colonists formed communities and developed educational practices according to their special visions of the pious life and of the good society.[16] Before long, two patterns became discernible in colonial America with respect to the proper role of political authorities in education. One position was that the government had a legitimate responsibility to encourage, support, and direct education. This arrangement was only possible, however, in religiously homogeneous settlements or in a political setting in which one group controlled the government and could use the power of the state to impose its world view through education on all students. In this framework a civil-religious order came to expression in established schools as well as in an established church.

Other groups, however, took the position that the government should play only an indirect role, if any at all, in education. In a few of the colonies, especially those that demonstrated greater religious diversity, education was the responsibility of more than one group, none of which had sufficient political power to impose its view of life on all schools by political means. Thus the conviction grew, more as a result of historical circumstances than as a matter of principle, that government should not control education or perhaps even support schools at all.

Puritan New England was an example of the first type of educational pattern. In the Puritan settlements the central concern for establishing a Christian commonwealth was clearly reflected in the way government took an active role in supporting education. In 1642 the Massachusetts General Court enacted the first of a series of laws designed to encourage education. Municipal officials in every settlement were required to insure the children's "ability to read and understand the principles of religion and the capitall lawes of the country."[17] It was not long before every family and town was required to provide a minimum of education for every child.[18] From its inception Massachusetts Bay was a commonwealth with an educational spirit, a true *paideia*; education played a central role in the Puritan vision of culture building.[19]

The role of the family was still primary in the early education of Puritan children. Although the early laws which established schools specified the need for literacy and job training, they did not require compulsory schooling outside the family. The family fulfilling its obligations to its children remained the center of the educational process. The state became involved in primary education only because parents began to neglect their duty to teach their children to read, to catechize them, and to train them for useful employment. Thus, the first schools were organized because the saints feared "the great neglect of many parents and masters in training up their children in learning and labor, and other implyments which may be proffitable to the common wealth."[20]

In the Puritan covenantal community, citizenship was limited to the elect, to full church members. Recognition of an individual's civil rights (voting, holding public office, and so on) was contingent upon that person's membership in the covenant of grace and the church covenant. Those individuals who were not of the elect but who nevertheless resided in the commonwealth were referred to as the "inhabitants." Inhabitants were required by law to pay taxes, attend the Puritan church, and obey the civil laws instituted by the elect, but they were excluded from the privileges of active citizenship. Only the elect were citizens. Since all education had to conform to the standards of the Puritan religion, the inhabitants were thus required to provide financial support not only for a church but also for schools that did not necessarily reflect or express their own views of life. The realities of Puritan civil religion were thus restrictive for all those that stood outside of the Puritan mainstream.

By the end of the seventeenth century the homogeneous religious character of Massachusetts Bay had disappeared. The saints had lost their full political control. But even before the demise of the Puritan experiment, the efforts of the General Court to raise the standards and tighten the enforcement of laws pertaining to public education were meeting with resistance.[21] Bailyn indicates that the Puritan ideal of an equal minimum of education for everyone "could not be maintained beyond the early period of religious enthusiasm and past the boundaries of the original clustering settlements."[22] The increasing size, diversity, and scattering of the population, the political instability occasioned by the colonial wars, and the continual shortage of public funds meant that support for education of the Puritan variety was limited indeed.[23] The waves of revivalism throughout the eighteenth century produced many schools, colleges, and academies, but they were the products of denominational interest and competition. Thus, the development of a statewide system of common schools would have to await the emergence of new ideas, new leadership, and new social conditions in the early nineteenth century.[24]

The second form of educational arrangement, in which the state played a very limited role in education, was the characteristic pattern in the middle and southern colonies. The failure to achieve the same level of educational establishment as in Massachusetts Bay was largely the result of the diversified religious character of these colonies rather than an indication of a lack of Quaker, Lutheran, Catholic, Dutch Reformed, or Anglican concern for education.

In Pennsylvania, for example, the Quakers found themselves in a curious predicament. On the one hand they were the proprietory party in the colony and were committed to Quaker education as an expression of true piety. On the other hand, they were heirs of the Protestant movements that championed religious freedom. The dilemma was resolved only by the exigencies of history.

Despite William Penn's original plan that the "Governor and Provincial Council shall erect and order all public schools," a common system of education could not be implemented in a colony that was so religiously pluralistic.[25] J. P. Wickersham has demonstrated that there is little evidence of public support for education in the records of the proprietors, the governors, the Provincial Council, or the General Assembly from Penn's time up to the outbreak of the Revolutionary War.[26] Penn himself seems to have decided, however reluctantly, to abandon his original idea concerning the relationship of state and schools in the face of the diverse religious opinions throughout the colony. In the last "Charter of Privileges," which was granted by Penn in 1701 and which continued in force until the adoption of the constitution of 1776, there was no mention of education. Wickersham concludes that without doubt Penn "intended to make education universal throughout the Province by public authority," but Pennsylvania "was so distracted by clashing principles, intestine feuds and warring factions" that the original plan was impossible to carry out.[27]

Pennsylvania did not follow the Puritan example of using the power of the state to attempt to propagate one particular world view through the schools. According to Lawrence Cremin, it was in the Pennsylvania experience that for "the first time in earnest . . . Americans had to contend with the dilemmas of public education in a pluralistic society."[28] Although the situation evolved more as a matter of historical circumstances than as a consequence of a conviction about what ought to be the proper relationship between the state and the schools in a pluralistic society, education in colonial Pennsylvania remained the responsibility of families and of the different religious communities.[29]

A similar relationship between government and schools characterized much of the South. In the case of Virginia, for example, the early government attempts to support education met with failure. The reason for the failure was not that the original colony was merely a commercial enterprise backed by the Virginia Company of London. Perry Miller reminds us of the extent to which a religious motive was behind the establishment of the colony by pointing out that within Virginia originally "the government was formed by a conscious and powerful intention to merge the Society with the purposes of God."[30] The Anglicans of Virginia were no less concerned than the Quakers of Pennsylvania or the Puritans of Massachusetts that their society, including education, should reflect the values of a particular way of life. Indeed, from the beginning of the Virginia colony in 1607, repeated attempts were made to educate both young Indians and the children of the settlers.[31] But neither the original efforts of James I to erect in Virginia "some churches and schools for the education of the children of those [Indian] barbarians" nor the first plans of the Virginia Company to build a public free school "for the education of children and grounding of them in the principles of religion, civility of life and humane learning" were successful.[32]

Those early attempts by the governing authorities in Virginia to support education were followed by other equally unsuccessful attempts. The continued failures can be traced, in part, to two causes. First, Virginia became the home of different ethnic and religious groups, as did Pennsylvania. In addition to the Anglicans there were Huguenots, German Protestants, Presbyterians, Quakers, Catholics, and others that settled in Virginia. To impose a uniform system of public education on such a diverse population could present enormous problems. A second cause for the failure was Virginia's plantation economy. Because the population was spread out on plantations and farms, it was extremely difficult to impose any type of uniformity. To a large extent the diverse population and the plantation system shaped the direction of Virginia's educational system and kept it from developing along the lines of that in Puritan New England.

In time what emerged in Virginia was state supported education only for some poor and orphaned children. In the same year as the famous Massachusetts statue of 1642, Anglican Virginia ordered its county officials to "take up" children of disabled parents "to maintaine and educate them."[33] Those families who could pay sent their children to private tutors or private schools, while poor children had to do without schooling if they were not among the fortunate few to receive free public education. For the great majority of children whose parents did not provide educational opportunities there was no alternative. This remained the case in much of the South well into the nineteenth century.

The political structures of colonial America contained, for the most part, the essential characteristics of the European civil-religious establishments that took shape following the religious wars of the Reformation period. The old world had been left behind, but the colonists made their own attempts to keep the new political communities glued together by means of an enforced confessional homogeneity. Established churches were one of the means many of the colonies used to accomplish this goal. But closely associated with both church and state in the effort to nurture social homogeneity were the schools.

Schools have been and remain fundamentally important institutions for the identity and continuity of a people, whether that people understands itself as a "religious, covenant people" or as an "independent political people." Colonial America displayed a variety of means of providing for education. But the question that grew in importance during the eighteenth century, the period when established churches were slowly losing both their political control and their special privileges within the colonies, concerned the responsibility of the government for schools. If a uniform ecclesiastical confession could no longer provide the social glue for a political community, then how could that society be held together as a moral and human community? Would it be necessary for the states to set up schools to instruct everyone in the common way of good republican citizenship? If so, would there be any difference between a civil-religious order that came to expression in a church establishment and a civil-religious order that manifested itself in an educational establishment?

CHAPTER 2

THE REPUBLICAN VISION OF THOMAS JEFFERSON

THE historical events of the Revolutionary period in America were also the events that laid the foundation for the civil-religious and educational patterns of American life that exist today. The key historical events were the Revolutionary War itself, the confederation of the independent states, the eventual federation of the republic under the Constitution of 1789, and the internalizing of democratic ideals in the early national period. One of the central figures in this period was Thomas Jefferson, whose vision of the republic, of freedom, and of education is at the center of the contemporary understanding of the place and meaning of schools in America. To understand American education and civil religion we must understand Jefferson.

In this chapter and the next we will examine Jefferson's perspective and influence, along with that of some of his contemporaries. First, we will look at his philosophy of life in the broadest sense; that is, we will try to understand his basic convictions about human nature, God, and the world. Second, we will carefully analyze the meaning of "religion" as Jefferson understood it. Then in Chapter Three we will give an account of his political philosophy, directing special attention to Jefferson's conception of civil rights and religious freedom within the public legal order. Finally, we will look at Jefferson's conception of the place and task of education in the republic, pointing to the significance of this perspective for the political-educational structures that were to be established in the nineteenth century.

JEFFERSON'S GENERAL PHILOSOPHIC OUTLOOK

Thomas Jefferson, the botanical expert, architectural designer, experimental inventor, political leader, and intellectual enthusiast, is not usually remembered as a religious philosopher. His

15

thinking about God and religion was, in fact, neither original nor unique. Nevertheless, as Robert Healey points out, "Jefferson's belief that a particular kind of God had created a particular kind of universe and a particular kind of man is the logical basis of the rest of his thought."[1]

What kind of thinker was Jefferson? Without doubt he was an Enlightenment rationalist in his deepest convictions about God, humanity, and the world, and the chief outlines of his thought provide an adequate summary of Enlightenment faith.

First of all, Jefferson returned to the classical Latin philosophers, especially to the Stoics, for his outlook on life. Not that Jefferson was a classical scholar, but as he matured he left behind the orthodox Christianity of his youth and built up a moralistic, patriotic religion of personal goodness and dedication to public duty, very similar to the religion of Cicero. Peter Gay summarizes Jefferson's stance as an Enlightenment figure this way:

> Machiavelli and Bolingbroke confirmed [for Jefferson] what he had learned in Cicero's *Tusculan Disputations*: contempt for the fear of death, contempt for "superstition," admiration for sturdy pagan self-reliance. It was from Bolingbroke that he copied this sentence: while the system of Christ is doubtful and incomplete, "A system thus collected from the writings of ancient heathen moralists, of Tully, of Seneca, of Epictetus, and others, would be more full, more entire, more coherent, and more clearly deduced from unquestionable principles of knowledge." Nothing displays the family resemblance among all branches of the Western Enlightenment more strikingly than this earnest entry in a young colonial's commonplace book; the heathen sentiment from Bolingbroke, intellectual parent to Voltaire as much as to Jefferson, went back, like many such sentiments, to a common root: classical Latinity.[2]

Jefferson's religion was essentially a moral philosophy. God functioned in this moral philosophy, not as the historical Lord of Abraham, Isaac, and Jacob, not as the father of Jesus Christ, head of the church and Lord of the world, but as the benevolent creator who preserves humans in this life and judges the moral worth of each person after death. The center of gravity in such a world is not God but the moral life of human beings. Jefferson could advise his nephew, Peter Carr, for example, to take up the critical reading of the Bible, not in order to learn a specially revealed truth from God, but to see how much of this rather "human" book could pass the rational and moral test for truth. "Do not be frightened from this inquiry," advised Uncle Thomas, "by any fear of its consequences":

If it ends in a belief that there is no God, you will find incitements to virtue in the comfort and pleasantness you feel in its exercise, and the love of others which it will procure you. If you find reason to believe there is a God, a consciousness that you are acting under his eye, and that he approves you, will be a vast additional incitement; if that there be a future state, the hope of a happy existence in that increases the appetite to deserve it; if that Jesus was also a god, you will be comforted by a belief of his aid and love.[3]

The satisfaction of such a religion, as one can see here, is in the "incitement to virtue," the feelings of "comfort and pleasantness," the "appetite" for doing good that a person can obtain from the rational conclusions of a careful empirical inquiry. Whether or not God exists, whether or not Jesus is a God — these are incidental questions whose solutions have value only in terms of their usefulness for the moral life of human beings. In an important sense such questions need not even be answered; or at least it is relatively inconsequential whether they are answered positively or negatively. As Jefferson wrote to John Adams, my religion "is known to my God and myself alone. Its evidence before the world is to be sought in my life; if that has been *honest* and *dutiful* to society, the religion which has regulated it cannot be a bad one."[4]

Another important feature of Jefferson's "enlightened" view of life is his understanding of human life as animal life. Human creatures constitute a unique species of animal "whose humanity lay in . . . physical needs and physical attributes." The needs must be satisfied while the attributes are developed; "from these propositions Jefferson derived his doctrine of man."[5] Jefferson's anthropology, which regards humans as sophisticated, physical animals, stands in the line of modern thinkers from John Locke through the Enlightenment rationalists and Common Sense philosophers.[6] Moreover, the physical needs and attributes of the human animal require a special kind of adaptation and ingenuity in order to enable individuals of the same species to live and work together. This species has to create a social life designed to facilitate the satisfaction of every person's needs. For Jefferson nothing could be clearer than that the creator who made human beings with needs "intended all men to achieve satisfaction of their needs in the world in which He had placed them."[7] Thus humans came to accept the moral responsibility of creating a social arrangement capable of satisfying the physical needs of each individual.

Jefferson's view of human nature combines a physical, biological explanation of the world (including many species of animals, one of which is human) with a strong doctrine of human moral responsibility. This understanding of life is Jefferson's philosophy—a philosophy shared with many others of his day. This philosophy was also his religion; it provided the framework and the content of his belief in and relationship to the author of nature.

One of the linchpins of Jefferson's moral philosophy was his faith in "reason." Certainly Jefferson had no faith in abstract reason or in speculative reason—reason as a source of truth and ideas in itself. But Jefferson did put his trust in experimental, empirical reason, the kind of intellectual faculty that worked carefully with the "facts." Reason, for Jefferson, was even the ultimate judge of true religion, because in the deepest sense reason was Jefferson's religious guide and Lord. In his *Notes on the State of Virginia* Jefferson confessed, "Reason and free inquiry are the only effectual agents against error. Give a loose to them, they will support the true religion by bringing every false one to their tribunal, to the test of their investigation. They are the natural enemies of error, and of error only."[8] Jefferson's advice to nephew Peter Carr includes the challenge to "Fix reason firmly in her seat, and call to her tribunal every fact, every opinion. Question with boldness even the existence of a God; because, if there be one, he must more approve of the homage of reason, than that of blindfolded fear."[9]

It is striking here that Jefferson appears supremely confident in reason and its ability to be the self-sustaining judge of truth, even if God does not exist. At the same time, if God *does* exist, Jefferson is supremely confident of knowing exactly the "rational" preferences and desires of that God. Once again we are confronted directly with the *faith* of an Enlightenment rationalist. As Carl Becker observes, "The eighteenth century did not abandon the old effort to share in the mind of God; it only went about it with greater confidence, and had at last the presumption to think that the infinite mind of God and the finite mind of man were one and the same thing."[10] Whether or not God exists, reason is supreme and one can be rational if one chooses. The finite mind, then, can be in touch with, and is an expression of, that which is the supreme and ultimate order of the universe. To be rational is to be certain, to be right, to be human, to be moral, to be in touch with the true order of nature and nature's God. Jefferson's writings, consequently, always stress the contrast between reason or rationality and an opposite something that is wholly unacceptable. "Opinion," "superstition," "fear," "novelty," "fraud"—all of these are clearly the opposite of reason and her offspring.[11] To be fully human, one must follow reason, not opinion or superstition or novelty.

Reason, which supposedly uncovers the factual truth of the universe, is thus at the heart of Jefferson's faith. But despite Jefferson's practical empirical rationalism, his faith rests in more than scientific or intellectual reason. Rationality, for Jefferson, is also a *moral* ideal. Reason guides people in the direction that they *ought* to go. Rationality is the source of and guide to social order and harmony. Reason does not simply describe the "facts" of the physical universe; it also prescribes what ought to be and how human beings ought to live as nature's moral agents.

John Dewey emphasized this point years ago. Jefferson's view of life is moral through and through, observed Dewey. And morality to Jefferson indicates what is rational and natural: "To put ourselves in touch with Jefferson's position we have therefore to translate the word 'natural' into *moral*."[12] In other words, when Jefferson talks about nature or the laws of nature or nature's God, or about reason and the rational order of the universe, he is not talking about the physical, biological, psychological world alone; he is also talking about a moral universe in which the human animal *ought* to learn to live by reason in order to live in tune with the dictates of nature for the human species.

Another key term in understanding Jefferson's Enlightenment faith is *conscience* or the *moral sense*. Conscience is the human faculty by means of which nature and conviction authoritatively impress upon the individual the demands of duty to God and to fellow humans.[13] Of course, conscience or the moral sense should testify to what is rational. Jefferson, however, believes that the moral sense is autonomous, since not everyone does in fact think rationally or understand the dictates of nature and reason. Even though reason is the only sure guide to truth, Jefferson believes that every person (not just the philosopher) can "sense" or "feel" what is morally right by a direct, unreflective intuition. Thus, he treats conscience as a sixth "sense," independent of thinking, an intuitive receptor of moral guidance that no one can escape. In a letter to Thomas Law, Jefferson expresses his surprise that so many people could have differing opinions about the nature of the common moral sense which the creator implanted in all human creatures, making it "so much a part of our constitution as that no errors of reasoning or of speculation might lead us astray from its observation in practice."[14]

On the one hand, therefore, Jefferson starts from the observed "fact" that people do not all think rationally and correctly according to his assumed standard of what is rational. They do not all agree about the true order of nature or share the same opinions. It is necessary, in Jefferson's view, to be able to count on some sense within human nature by which everyone will "feel" what is universally right and good. On the other hand, Jefferson is confident that some people (including himself) can know what the rational foundation of morality really is. The truly rational person not only shares the universal moral sense with everyone else but also is able to rise above the clash of conflicting opinions, superstitions, and novel thoughts that belong to the minds of the mass of humankind in order to discover the unity and congruence of reason, conscience, and nature. In fact, the morally sensitive, rationally disciplined person is in a position to help shape and discipline the moral habits and consciences of others in accord with the truth.

Within the context of Jefferson's thinking about God, humanity, and nature we can now give a brief account of the feature of his general philosophy that is perhaps most important for his social and political ideas. This is the doctrine of "natural rights."

The ancient Stoics conceived of the order of the universe as an eternal, rational, moral law-order. Human beings, in other words, could find and understand their place and identity in the world by coming to an understanding of the rational *natural law*. This philosophy was revived and enjoyed great influence between the Renaissance and the Enlightenment, and it had a tremendous impact on Jefferson by way of John Locke and Scottish Common Sense philosophy. Becker provides a valuable background description of this development, pointing to the general influence of Locke as a transmitter of the modernized Stoic outlook:

> Locke, more perhaps than any one else, made it possible for the eighteenth century to believe what it wanted to believe: namely, that in the world of human relations as well as in the physical world, it was possible for men to "correspond with the general harmony of Nature"; that since man, and the mind of man, were integral parts of the work of God, it was possible for man, by the use of his mind, to bring his thought and conduct, and hence the institutions by which he lived, into a perfect harmony with the Universal Natural Order. In the eighteenth century, therefore, these truths were widely accepted as self evident: that a valid morality would be a "natural morality," a valid religion would be a "natural religion," a valid law of politics would be a "natural law." This was only another way of saying that morality, religion, and politics ought to conform to God's will as revealed in the essential nature of man.[16]

Even Garry Wills (who challenges Becker's assumption that Locke's general influence on the Enlightenment is sufficient to explain Jefferson's political philosophy) does not try to prove that Locke was not influential on Jefferson. Wills argues simply that the impact of Scottish Common Sense philosophy on Jefferson must be considered preeminent.[17]

Jefferson saw important connections combining the will of God, the order of nature, and the essential nature of human beings. God is rational; nature is rational; humans are rational. God's will is revealed not through any special unnatural revelations but simply through human nature and the rest of the universe. What a person discovers about himself and his natural, rational morality is the whole truth about human nature, just as one's scientific discovery of the order of nature is the whole truth about the non-human world. But if a rational explanation of everything is sufficient, if it provides an exhaustive account of all that exists, then there is no other "will of God" that could possibly transcend or remain hidden from human beings. The consequence of this line of thought is that nature, including its human beings, becomes deified; or to put it the other way around, God is fully rationalized and naturalized.[18]

By Jefferson's time, therefore, the old Stoic natural law philosophy had become a natural rights doctrine. It was a tenet of Enlightenment faith that nature's laws for human beings actually inhere in each individual and in the moral sense as a natural right. Take, for example, those familiar phrases of the Declaration of Independence penned by Jefferson:

> We hold these truths to be self-evident, that all men are created equal; that they are endowed by their Creator with certain unalienable rights; that among these are life, liberty and the pursuit of happiness. That, to secure these rights, governments are instituted among men, deriving their just powers from the consent of the governed.

Jefferson's appeal here (for a ground of firm truth and authority) is neither to God nor to God's eternal law nor to the Bible. It is simply to what is "self-evident" within the mind and common conscience of humanity; it is an appeal to the universal, rational/moral essence of human nature that corresponds to the true order of nature, which is God's will.

The universal testimony of the truth within a person is not merely that of an external order of nature but is the testimony of each person's inalienable rights. These *natural rights*, understood through simple, intuitive self-evidence without any need to appeal beyond the inner testimony of conscience and reason, are the sole basis for the powers and obligations of a government, according to Jefferson. The creator endows individuals with rights; he does not have anything to do with the creation of government or with the defining of its normative structure, limits, and tasks.

With nature, reason, conscience, and natural rights on such a firm footing, surely it is easy to understand how Jefferson could have been relatively unconcerned about the existence or nonexistence of a traditional deity. His deepest faith was in human reason and conscience as the judge of the truth. If nature has a God, fine; he will know his place. If reason does not find sufficient evidence for God's existence, fine; the self-sufficient world of nature and reason are enough to give firm direction to human moral life.

THE MEANING OF RELIGION FOR JEFFERSON

The place and meaning of religion in Jefferson's thought presents two aspects. On the one hand Jefferson appears quite irreligious. He remained unconvinced about a number of Christian doctrines; he was an Enlightenment materialist and naturalist; he was quite willing to base morality on natural reason and the moral sense without feeling an absolute necessity for belief in God; he was a moral philosopher, not a theologian or churchman in the traditional sense. On the other hand, we have seen that Jefferson approached nature and reason quite religiously. He had faith in reason; he did believe in nature's God; and morality was religion for Jefferson. Obviously, then, we must come to a sharper definition of "religion" in Jefferson's thought if we are to understand his political philosophy, which included the principle of religious freedom.

In a letter written in 1809, Jefferson makes the following statement that substantially clarifies his religious position and circumscribes the nature of the problem we have just raised:

> Reading, reflection and time have convinced me that the interests of society require the observation of those moral precepts only in which all religions agree . . . and that we should not intermeddle with the particular dogmas in which all religions differ, and which are totally unconnected with morality. . . . The practice of morality being necessary for the well-being of society, he [the Creator] has taken care to impress its precepts so indelibly on our hearts that they shall not be effaced by the subtleties of our brain.[19]

First, note that Jefferson's idea of the purpose of religion's good precepts is the enhancement of human morality and the well-being of society. Human beings do not exist for the sake of God and religious service, but rather religion and God function to encourage human welfare. Certainly, therefore, Jefferson was not opposed to religion. To the contrary, he was interested in articulating a principle by which true and significant religion could be recognized. And in his case, the criterion was a rational, utilitarian one—the usefulness of religion for the individual and society.

Second, Jefferson makes it clear that the only kind of religion that passes the test of social and moral utility is the religion of universal morality. True religion, in other words, is nothing but universal morality; it is "the response of healthy and reasonable men to needs determined by general interest and social utility."[20] Only those moral precepts in which *all* religions agree, says Jefferson, are necessary for society to observe. The "particular dogmas" upon which religions differ, specifically those that are not directly connected to morality, are of no concern to society as a whole. They are, in all probability, wrong, and in any case they are socially irrelevant. Moral, socially relevant religion is universal morality—nothing more, nothing less.

Third, Jefferson's confession in his letter to Fishback reveals how we are able to discern this true religion of socially useful universal morality. The creator has impressed universal moral precepts on the human conscience in such an indelible way that not even the variety of opinions that arise in people's minds can alter these moral convictions. As we pointed out earlier, Jefferson recognized a variety of "opinions," "beliefs," and "ideas" among people. The independence that he granted to conscience or the moral sense was due to his belief that morality is and would remain universal, unvarying even amidst the variety of brain structures and opinions. Moreover, the common universal moral precepts, rather than peculiar and diverse opinions, bear testimony to what is the rational and natural order.

David Little summarizes the three points above in a succinct fashion when he says:

> As in everything else, the sure standard of the moral sense is the only norm for evaluating what is useful and what is beside the point in all religious traditions. By that standard, naturally, the only aspect of religion worth salvaging is the common moral core. The leftover dogmas and superstitions may safely be humored by an enlightenment society until they blow away in the wind, with the rest of the theories.[21]

It is a fair question how Jefferson's view of true religion squares with the religious "facts" of his day and with the views of other people. In other words, was there universal agreement among the Americans of Jefferson's day on a core of moral principles? What about those religious groups that did take their "dogmas" seriously? Were they willing to grant that their own "particular dogmas" were secondary to universal morality or perhaps even wrong? And if not, how are we to judge between Jefferson's religion (which then was not universal) and the religions of those groups that were not followers of Jeffersonian rationalism?

In the light of these questions, it becomes clear that Jefferson's letter of 1809 is really a statement of hope, faith, and what ought to be — it was a new ecumenical ideal. Jefferson recognized that the variety of human opinions would probably continue to frustrate any ultimate agreement on many issues. He fondly hoped that some human faculty other than the brain (namely, the moral sense) would bear testimony to what was morally universal, rational, and natural for religious belief. But even in respect to the moral precepts of humanity, Jefferson could really only say, as he admitted elsewhere, that "What all agree in, is probably right. What no two agree in, most probably wrong."[22]

But what precisely do all agree in? And do all agree that only what is universally agreed among them *ought* to be believed? And what about those doctrines that more than two agree in but which are not believed universally? Jews and Christians, for example, do not both believe in the Trinity, though both believe in God. Most Christians were quite unwilling in Jefferson's day, as now, to give up their faith in the "peculiar dogma" of the Trinity. Jefferson, of course, thought that just such a doctrine ought to be dismissed, and he had relinquished it. But this only demonstrates that Jefferson's own idea of the true religion was not universal, even though it was one that he thought ought to be universalized.[23]

Healey indicates that Jefferson's religion was based on what we might call a "common core" of religious belief, "a group of tenets on which all sects could be expected to agree." This core did not include "creed or dogma," says Healey, "but it did most certainly embrace the field of morality and also the rational or philosophic proofs of the existence of God."[24] What we have here, however, is nothing more than Jefferson's confession of the Stoically rooted Enlightenment faith — a faith in universal, natural, moral religion, which he insists should be the only true religion.[25] In fact, however, not everyone in America and Europe, much less in the rest of the world, was an Enlightenment deist.[26]

Furthermore, many, if not most, Christians did not agree

with Jefferson that religion serves chiefly a utilitarian function for personal and social welfare. Nor would most religious groups of Jefferson's day have agreed that only the universal moral elements in all religions constitute the true religion. And clearly not everyone in Jefferson's day was willing to admit that a universal moral conscience exists apart from the diversity of minds, opinions, and special revelations.

But perhaps what is even more significant, Jefferson's religion was not a moral system exclusively; it included some important "particular dogmas" not directly related to morality. Consider, for example, Jefferson's conviction that the true religion of morality is a rational and natural religion independent of any special revelation. Surely this conviction is much more than a precept of the moral sense. Jefferson here articulates an argument, in fact a belief, that true religion cannot have any supernatural revelation as its source. Nature, reason, and conscience are sufficient for moral religion.[27] But not everyone agreed with Jefferson. Almost all the Christian churches stood on the firm conviction that apart from the special revelation of Christ and the scriptures true religion cannot exist.

What can we say then to Jefferson? Is the affirmation or denial of special revelation merely a moral precept of social utility, or is it a "dogma" over which people are divided, thus making it impossible for any universal religion to exist? Is the conviction about the validity of special revelation a conviction of the moral conscience only, or also of reason? Jefferson's rejection of special revelation was not, in fact, a universally accepted core precept, nor did it enjoy the simple and universal moral assent of all. The naturalistic rejection of revelation is, however, an integral part of Jefferson's whole philosophy, which cannot stand if peculiar and special revelations are admitted as possible. Jefferson, therefore, is not simply reporting the facts of reality when he writes about the only true and universal religion. To the contrary, he is involved in urging upon others (evangelistically proclaiming to them) a specific religious commitment and faith that entails conversion and the rejection of other religious faiths.

And what happens if other religious groups refuse to accept Jefferson's gospel? The logical conclusion is that they will have to be excommunicated, at least in principle, from the universal community of moral humanity, from the only true religion. In fact Jefferson is explicit in this regard with respect to Calvin and his followers. Calvin and the Calvinists, says Jefferson, are not participants in the true religion; they must be viewed as atheists. In a letter to John Adams in 1823, Jefferson explained:

I can never join Calvin in addressing *his* God. He was indeed an atheist, which I can never be; or rather his religion was daemonism. If ever man worshiped a false God, he did. The Being described in his five points, is not the God whom you and I acknowledge and adore, the Creator and benevolent Governor of the world; but a daemon of malignant spirit. It would be more pardonable to believe in no God at all, than to blaspheme Him by the atrocious attributes of Calvin. Indeed, I think that every Christian sect gives a great handle to atheism by their general dogma, that, without a revelation, there would not be sufficient proof of the being of a God.[28]

Jefferson does not engage in any examination of the biblical evidence that Calvin used, in order to try to show that the biblical texts were illegitimate or that Calvin had misinterpreted the material. Jefferson does not engage in philosophic or scientific argument to show why the biblical (and other) materials used by Calvin ought to be rejected as evidence. No, he simply puts Calvin's idea of God alongside his own rational, moral idea and concludes with utmost sectarian dogmatism that Calvin's God must go. Nor does Jefferson's attack stop at Calvin. All Christian sects tend to insist upon revelation to some extent. They go beyond what is available to the common moral sense of everyone and thus simply give encouragement to atheists.

The meaning of religion for Jefferson is clear. He was indeed a religious believer, neither nonreligious nor irreligious. But his religion was a very definite, particular religion — the religion of Enlightenment rationalism that entailed the fundamental principles of (1) social/moral utility as its purpose, (2) universal morality as its chief content, (3) the "moral sense" as its infallible receptor, and (4) antirevelational rationalism as its discriminating judge of truth.[29] Dogmas other than the above Jefferson identifies as the products of the singular, novel, individual, and sometimes fraudulent "opinions" of people who do not limit themselves to the universal testimony of moral conscience but dogmatically build up "creeds" and "doctrines" on the basis of their own private ideas of "revelations" that are not rational or natural. From Jefferson's standpoint it is necessary to acknowledge the existence of churches and sects that are constituted upon such foundations, just as one has to acknowledge the existence of a variety of opinions among people as a consequence of the peculiar structure of each person's mind. But the beliefs of such sects and churches and individuals cannot, from Jefferson's point of view, be admitted as valid for the moral and religious foundations of society in the universal community of humanity.

The fact that the naturalistic religion of Enlightenment rationalism was not universal in Jefferson's day did not diminish his conviction that it ought to become universal. To the extent he believed his to be the only true religion, Jefferson was simply advancing, as an evangelist, a particular religion rooted in the Enlightenment ideal of a universal, rational humanity. Moreover, he advanced this religion over against the Christian religion, which had become thoroughly fragmented among competing groups of Protestants and Catholics that excluded one another and still excluded Jews. Jefferson hoped that his religion would bring *all* people together in a moral community on the basis of what was common among them.

The clear implication is that Jefferson's religion could become universal (and not exclusive) only if other claims to "true religion" were gradually dropped. Short of that, however, Jefferson's religion could function as the universal common denominator, in the public realm if all other religious groups admitted to its authority while remaining satisfied to hold on to their own peculiar dogmas in a limited, private, nonuniversal realm. If other religions would fade away entirely after their members were converted to the Jeffersonian religion, then clearly Jefferson's hope would be fulfilled. But Jefferson's hope would be realized almost as fully if other religions were to admit that it was *not* necessary for them to dominate and guide the universal order of humanity in an institutional and structural way, and that they were willing to live as peculiar "sects" among other peculiar "sects" in an equal fashion, each recognizing in Jefferson's common rational morality the framework which could integrate them all in a universal order. Each religious group would then be free to hold its private dogmas without coercive support or impairment, while Jeffersonians would be free to organize the universal order on a common, rational, moral basis in the hope that gradually the peculiar "opinions" of the sects would wither away under exposure to the light of reason.[30]

The word *religion*, then, has two references or meanings in Jefferson's thinking. It can identify the true faith of rational, natural morality which is the universal truth. Or *religion* can be used with reference to the groups and sects of Christians, Jews, and others that hold on to their own, differing dogmas and creeds. Obviously, in the first sense religion has very positive connotations for Jefferson, while in the second sense the word has distinctly negative connotations.[31]

One might imagine that Jefferson and his fellow rationalists had quite a difficult time convincing Christians of this distinction in the meaning of religion. However, such was not the case.[32] In the first place the Christian churches and groups thought of themselves as *religious* groups. They held their religion as their most important identifying characteristic. In their usage, *religion* was the term that referred to their special creedal, ecclesiastical, and personal commitments. And they were aware of the fact that a number of different religious "sects," "churches," and groups existed.

By contrast, Jefferson's natural, rational, universal morality had no ecclesiastical identification and usually did not even go by the name *religion*. It was, of course, as we have seen, a "natural religion," but Jefferson made very little of the word *religion* to identify it. The key identifying adjectives for his faith are "moral," "rational," "natural," and so forth. Thus Jefferson's natural religion was regarded not so much as a competing religion but as a philosophy for universal, moral order among all people, while the word *religion* continued to refer to the various religious groups other than the Enlightenment rationalists.

Second, most of the Christian groups saw their special religious doctrines and practices as wholly individual matters, involving their relationship to God, their personal relationships locally and in the home, and the condition of their souls. It was not at all strange for them to expect that in the larger realm of social and political order some general, universal moral principles ought to hold. The public political arena was viewed by many Christians as a primarily "secular" (this-worldly, *not* religious), rational, and natural arena. Thus Jefferson's principles for a universal morality could be accepted for that realm as long as they were perceived as part of a rational philosophy rather than as part of a new religion.

Jefferson, on the other hand, was concerned precisely with the public, political realm. The complex world of ecclesiastical and personal piety was of little interest to him. He was more than willing to have his religion accepted as a public moral philosophy since that is exactly what it was. Due to their own perspective, therefore, the churches and sects clearly did not understand that Jefferson's moral philosophy was a religion. While the religious groups held on to their different religious perspectives and allowed Jefferson's moral philosophy to fill the public void, Jefferson's religion was able thereby to become the public philosophy of the new nation.

Thus, the Christian groups reaffirmed their dualistic position in the world, accepting both their own particular religious perspective for private life as well as the common, public philosophy of Jefferson for their public, secular lives. Jefferson, however, stood fast with his integral, monistic view of life, discounting as useless and insignificant the "private" beliefs and "opinions" of the sects. The Christians held on to both religion *and* philosophy, religion *and* politics; Jefferson held a single philosophy of personal life and politics as an integral religious totality.

Finally, we should note that many Christian groups in early America were aware of the fact that their doctrinal and moral differences did and could continue to cause political conflict and turmoil when incorporated into the foundation of political order and civil rights. By the early part of the nineteenth century most religious groups in the United States, including the previously established churches, had been driven to the realization that another, more universal basis for religious freedom in the political order was needed than the one provided by the privileged establishment of one church. As long as they continued to identify "religion" with their diverse ecclesiastical groups, they could accept Jefferson's moral philosophy as a purely secular political instrument for public peace. The religious groups, not Jefferson, contributed the interpretative framework of a sacred (religious) and secular (not religious) duality in which the principles of nonecclesiastical, political life were seen as neutral, rational, and nonreligious. Jefferson, however, understood the principles of universal social and political life not as secular and neutral but as common, universal, moral, rational, and true; they were, very simply, the only principles which belonged to the true religion—the natural religion of universal, public morality.

CHAPTER 3

ADVOCATES OF A NEW ORDER FOR AMERICAN EDUCATION

THE PHILOSOPHY OF THE REPUBLIC

WITH Jefferson's view of life and religion before us, we may now turn to look at his understanding of the political order and the role that education should play within it.

The philosophy of natural rights and common moral sense that Jefferson inherited from the Enlightenment provides the general framework within which he developed his political philosophy. We have emphasized already one very important characteristic of this philosophy, namely, its view of a universal, inherent law of natural rights. In other words, all people everywhere are identical as to their inherent value and their position in nature. All possess the same right to life, liberty, and the pursuit of happiness, as Jefferson himself put it.

The other side of this legal and moral universalism, however, is the view of the *individual* as fundamentally unattached to any normative, divinely appointed social order. The individual possesses rights and an identity in relation to a universal law (the same as every other individual), but the universal legal and moral framework defines and supports nothing more than free, sovereign, unconnected individuals. Every *social* institution, every organization is built by free individuals who come together as independent persons to decide upon and organize the associations in which they want to live. Apart from autonomous individuals there is no prior normative framework of social obligations and duties which gives meaning and definition to human life. As Sidney Mead puts it, "All the lines of thinking of the eighteenth century converged on the idea of free, uncoerced, individual consent as the only proper basis for all man's organizations, civil and ecclesiastical."[1]

This individualistic/universalistic view of human nature meant that Jefferson possessed no real theory of the *state* as a distinct structure in society. We know that Jefferson developed an idea of how a government could be established by autonomous individuals, but he was unable to give an adequate account of that social institution called the state or political community within which the government functioned. The most that Jefferson could do, given his starting point, was to argue that every social institution is in principle a *voluntary society*.[2] But the argument that autonomous individuals are free to form voluntary societies provides no insight whatever into the character of, the distinction between, and the relationships among different kinds of voluntary societies. It does nothing to clarify the meaning of diverse social responsibilities among people, such as economic, political, and educational responsibilities.

Instead of a positive view of the structure and task of the state and its government, Jefferson posited essentially a negative view. That is, he made the case for what government ought *not* to do to free individuals, or at least how the government ought to be limited in what it does so that it will not inhibit free individuals. Boorstin skillfully summarizes this point:

> The Jeffersonian natural "rights" philosophy was thus a declaration of inability or unwillingness to give positive form to the concept of community, or to face the need for defining explicitly the moral ends to be served by government. From the point of view of the individual, "rights" have a positive enough look: they validate his power under certain circumstances and in certain ways to express his individuality without hindrance. But from the point of view of the community, "rights" have a negative implication: they prescribe what the community *cannot* do. They warn where government dare not go, without suggesting where it ought to go.[3]

Boorstin cites the problem of slavery in Jefferson's time, for example, to show that even though Jefferson was opposed to slavery as a "flagrant violation of the Creator's plan," he was uncertain what government should do about it for the sake of a just political community. He did not know how blacks should be treated if they were free. His abolitionism "was weakened because he was unsure what kind of community ought to emerge or what place the Negro should have in it."[4] Even though Jefferson considered blacks to be members of the single human species, his vision of the American nation could not quite contain them as an equal and free participants. Jefferson later suggested that blacks should be transported to foreign islands to colonize there.

Jefferson's political philosophy, then, assumes a universal natural and moral order in which individuals have autonomous rights. But given the abstract legal universalism and individualistic biological reductionism of this philosophy, it has proven to be a rather weak foundation for an adequate account of political life.

Part of the reason Jefferson did not sense the serious inadequacy of his political philosophy was that he did not really admit the serious problem of social and religious diversity in society. His proposal to ship Negroes to foreign islands is just one example of ignoring the problem of social diversity rather than solving it. The same was the case with the issue of religious plurality in the young nation. Jefferson's solution for "religious freedom," as we shall see, was less a proposal for integrating a true diversity into the public order than it was a means by which the diversity of strange and peculiar opinions could be shipped off into a nonpublic (if not foreign) backwater to make possible a homogeneous, nondifferentiated, universal association of free and rational individuals.

His picture of humanity was the Stoic ideal of a homogeneous, universal species of free, rational individuals. Those individuals were free to create a universal voluntary association with a set of common moral principles at its core and a government whose authority would be derived from the sovereignty of the individuals as a freely associating people. By definition, therefore, such a "body" or "people" could not be beset by those problems of social diversity that might exist if other loyalties (to the family, to the church, to the ethnic group, etc.) were ultimately significant in personal and social identity. No internal diversity could threaten this kind of homogeneous association.[5]

According to David Little, Jefferson overlooked the problems of competing loyalties and possible conflicts among different interpretations of life precisely because he was blindly convinced that all disputes about diverse religious, moral, and civic opinions would be overcome within the universal association of moral and rational individuals:

> Jefferson has implicit faith in the clarity and reliability of the moral sense of each individual, once its full powers are restored by government (among others), to direct men consistently and harmoniously to everyone's "greatest happiness." Consequently, he shows no concern, from the point of view of either the individual or the government, for the problem

of possible conflicts or tensions among different views of happiness, nor among different readings of the moral sense.[6]

It should be clear by now that Jefferson's universal moral association, identified essentially as the public political community or republic, was also, in his view, the true religious community of human beings. In this sense Jefferson did *not* have a philosophy of social and religious pluralism, even though he acknowledged the freedom and right of individuals who were members of the republic to form whatever voluntary associations they might choose. In the midst of many private associations Jefferson could recognize only one that represented the universal order of rational/moral/religious humanity, and that association was the non-pluralistic political association, or republic.

This interpretation, which may appear startling at first, is further confirmed by Jefferson's conception of the nature and structure of authority in the republic. The first moral principle of a republic, Jefferson argued, is that the will of the majority "is the fundamental law of every society of individuals of equal rights." The majority expresses the will of society even if that majority is decided by only a single vote. The only alternative to majority rule, Jefferson believed, is force, which must end in military despotism.[7] The principle of majority rule is the natural right for a "collection" of people just as the principle of free self-determination is the natural right of every individual. "Every man and every body of men on earth," said Jefferson, "possess the right of self-government. They receive it with their being from the hand of nature. Individuals exercise it by their single will; collections of men by that of their majority; for the law of the *majority* is the natural law for every society of men."[8] One can accept the concept of the "will of the people" and the "will of the majority" for a republic only by accepting the framework of Jefferson's natural rights philosophy as the true theology. Without accepting in large measure Jefferson's moral philosophy (natural religion), one cannot understand or accept these principles for society.

Jefferson's belief is not only that the moral conscience of every individual will guide the "whole people" to an undisputed consensus about the common happiness, but also that the majority of a people can speak with universal authority for the whole body on particular legislative matters within the republic. Of course, Jefferson wanted majority rule to go hand in hand with a respect for minority rights, but minority rights meant for him the rights of individuals to exercise their original autonomous freedom. He had no predisposition to believe that many diverse, minority communities *within* the republic might disagree with the direction in which the majority was leading the society. Within the realm of the public association — the republic — Jefferson did not envision pluralism; he saw only the majority rule of the *one*, undifferentiated association. Minority rights were inherent rights of individuals that the society as a whole (through its majority) could not infringe upon. Plurality existed only in that realm of the private, uncommon "opinions" of individuals and their nonpolitical voluntary associations. The great lesson Americans had to learn, Jefferson told William Bache in 1800, was to *"inculcate on minorities the duty of acquiescence in the will of the majority; and on majorities a respect for the rights of the minority."*[9]

The lack of a structural understanding of the state as a pluralistic community in Jefferson's thinking meant that the positive task of government within the republic was left (and remains) undefined. Even if religion could be adequately protected and encouraged as a strictly individual matter outside the public arena, that would still leave no guide for government action in relation to education, economic life, science and technology, western exploration and expansion, foreign affairs, and so forth. But precisely in these areas different views of life, along with different basic convictions about the nature of the republic, have come fully into the open during the past two centuries.

When Jefferson became President of the United States it became obvious to him that government could not be limited solely to the task of protecting individual rights; a republic needs definition as a social community: "He now easily presumed that whatever measures served prosperity or the 'needs' of the time must by definition serve the Creator's purpose."[10] Meeting needs in a pragmatic, utilitarian fashion thus became the uncritical definition of government's task in Jefferson's ill-conceived, homogeneous society of rational animals. But this course concealed still more dangers. In a letter to John B. Colvin in 1810 Jefferson made the following significant statement:

> A strict observance of the written laws is doubtless *one* of the high duties of a good citizen, but it is not the *highest*. The laws of necessity, of self-preservation, of saving our country when in danger, are of higher obligation. To lose our country by a scrupulous adherence to written law, would be to lose the law itself, with life, liberty, property and all those who are enjoying them with us; thus absurdly sacrificing the ends to the means.[11]

Jefferson's argument is that of *raison d'état*, the preeminence of the "national interest," which certainly implies that the end of preserving the republic (our country) must in some cases be sought by any means whatever. Moreover it implies that life, liberty, and property are privileges enjoyed by virtue of the republic's existence. Here is where the Jeffersonian *universalism*, connected as it is to the identity of the republic, actually takes precedence over the *individualism* at the other pole of his thinking. Mead observes that for Jefferson the limits of religious freedom (and we may add, every other freedom) are ultimately "defined by the 'public welfare.' "[12] The deeply religious character of Jefferson's republican philosophy is nowhere displayed so openly as here. The republic must be preserved at all costs, because it is the highest and final bearer of the moral hopes and legal rights to life, liberty, and property. Religious freedom is one of many freedoms defined and limited by this view of the public welfare. Since the republic has no prescribed direction or definition other than that it *not* inhibit the rights of individuals, it is free to move in any direction it chooses, by the will of its majority, for the meeting of needs and for its own preservation. If at any point there are doubts or disputes about the limits of "rights and freedoms" or about what the real "needs" are, they can be settled through appeal to the national interest. With Boorstin we can only ask the question, "What then could close the door to the subtle pragmatic arguments of men in power?"[13]

In very brief compass it is now possible to present the meaning of "religious freedom" for Jefferson. Religious freedom applied exclusively to "religion" in that narrower sense of diverse, uncommon dogmas, opinions, and beliefs of individuals and voluntary associations (churches) outside the universal, common, political association. Every private church, sect, and individual should be as free from political establishment or persecution as every other church, sect, or individual.[14] This freedom, however, is a freedom that can be exercised only individually or in a private association. With respect to religion, Jefferson believed that "the state should protect it precisely as it protects all other instruments for the formation of opinion—nothing more."[15] The homogeneous public political community with its majority rule, on the other hand, cannot accommodate in its own operation the diversity of opinions and beliefs held by individuals and private associations— precisely because that diversity has no place or meaning in the definition of the common, universal, public association of rational, moral individuals.[16]

From Jefferson's standpoint we can see that in the republic this meant the full and exclusive establishment of the only principles that have a right to organize *all* people in a common association, namely, the principles of (1) the autonomy and sovereignty of rational/moral individuals, and (2) the sovereignty of their majority in a homogeneous republic.[17] These principles, of course, stem directly from Jefferson's moral philosophy and natural religion, as we have seen.

Make no mistake about our interpretation of Jefferson at this juncture. Jefferson was not trying to impose by force his own materialistic convictions or his own belief that Christ was a man and not a god. He was not even trying to force people to confess his own belief that human beings are originally unconnected, autonomous individuals. Any individual is free in the privacy of his own "soul" or "brain" to believe what he wants to believe. But the public, *structural* implications coming from Jefferson's religious philosophy were in fact imposed on the republic as a whole. From Jefferson's religiously rooted world and life view there emerges the political structure for a new American civil religion which in time came to be imposed by law on all citizens. An individual can freely continue to believe, for example, that God is sovereign; or that divinely ordained social structures are normative for people and that individuals are not the autonomous authors of political society; or that the church ought to guide the state rather than be cut off from it. But these beliefs must have no public room to work themselves out in the structure of the Jeffersonian republic. Once the republic is established on the foundation of Enlightened, rationalistic principles, all other religions will thereafter have to remain "private" affairs of belief and opinion until the political structure of society is altered. Thus, as Sidney Mead points out, "Jefferson's theory implies that the limits even of religious freedom are to be defined by the 'public welfare!' "[18]

From the standpoint of those "religious" believers who treasure their special dogmas and convictions as the truth, we can see that the Jeffersonian principle of "religious freedom" means freedom from being either established or persecuted by the republic. It means freedom for individuals to keep believing and proclaiming their beliefs in *private* as long as they enter public life individually on the same basis as every other individual — the basis of those structural principles set down by the common Jeffersonian public philosophy (or moral religion). However, it also means the lack of public structural freedom within the republic to challenge the public philosophy on grounds that it is only one faith among many (and therefore ought not to be established). It means the lack of freedom fully to exercise one's faith (any faith other than Enlightenment rationalism) as an integral part of one's public participation in the republic. For the religious sects, churches, and individuals, in other words, "religious freedom" entails either (1) the ready acceptance of, and agreement to, a dualistic religion (of two religions, one public and one private), or (2) the uncomfortable compromise of living in the public arena on the basis of principles and procedures that contradict or are antagonistic to one's own religious convictions.[19]

In actuality, the almost universal attitude of the religious groups in Jefferson's time was the first of the alternatives noted above—namely, some kind of dualistic religious stance. This attitude predominated, according to Mead, because there was at the time a "general prevalence of rationalistic thinking and pietistic sentiment in the existing churches."[20] In other words, it was not Jefferson and the rationalists who forced the Christians (and others) against their wills to accept a divided life. The religious groups accepted the rationalist's proposal for religious freedom because, by and large, they had accepted a very limited view of their own "religions." They thought of religion as something private, existing alongside a so-called secular realm of life which they viewed as natural and nonreligious but which, in fact, was governed by the principles of Jefferson's very religious public philosophy.[21] "I conclude," says Mead, "that what is commonly called the relation between church and state in the United States ought to be resolved into the theological issue between the particularistic theological notions of the sects and the cosmopolitan, universal theology of the Republic."[22]

Jefferson's political theory (or theology, as Mead designates it), in the final analysis, contains the individualistic principles of majority rule and minority rights in the framework of what is supposed to be a morally homogeneous republic defined by the sovereignty of the people as a single, universal body. Religion, politics, education, and even liberty itself, however, become terms without any adequate structural definition for a society that was (and is) actually composed of different religious, ethnic, and linguistic communities and different social, cultural, and economic institutions.[23]

EDUCATION IN THE REPUBLIC

It follows naturally that Jefferson's understanding of the place and task of education does not accommodate a structural means of accounting for a diversity of educational outlooks. The individualism/universalism of his political philosophy entirely dominates his view of education.

The individualistic side of Jefferson's duality identifies education with the natural *capacity* of individuals to learn. Education is not a "natural right" but a natural capacity that individuals possess in varying degrees. For example, Jefferson entertained the suspicion that educational capacity was given to the different races in greater or lesser degree, and that the blacks "are inferior to the whites in the endowments both of body and mind."[24] The implication of this is that not all individuals can learn equally; those who are most gifted and capable should be allowed to develop their individual capacities as completely as possible, even though this means unequal education among all individuals.

The universalistic side of Jefferson's thought presumes that education ought to be the primary concern of the public body as a whole. Robert Heslep says that although Jefferson's proposals do not clearly reveal the "defining characteristics" of education, they do "indicate a conception of education's purpose for formal republican society."[25]

This individualistic/republicanistic duality manifests what David Tyack sees as Jefferson's concern for achieving a balance of *liberty* and *order* in society as a whole. Education is the key, the hope, the promise for ensuring the full development of individual liberty and freedom within a universal, homogeneous republic. While on the one hand education is supposed to develop each individual's different capacity in its own way, on the other hand education is nothing more than a political activity for securing uniformity, stability, and homogeneity in the public realm. Jefferson shared this perspective with his contemporaries, Noah Webster and Benjamin Rush:

> Not content with unconscious and haphazard socialization provided by family, political meeting, press, and informal associations, not trusting in the "givenness" of political beliefs and institutions, these men sought to instruct Americans deliberately in schools. Having fought a war to free the United States from one centralized authority, they attempted to create a new unity, a common citizenship and culture, and an appeal to a common future.[26]

Jefferson's conceptual framework for education is exactly parallel to his conceptual framework for religion. On the one side, in both cases, there is a diverse, even splintered and anarchic, individualism: each individual has his own opinions, his own beliefs, his own educational capacity, his own right to be free; each is and should remain autonomous, without any external authority controlling or directing him. On the other side there is that uniform, homogeneous, common universalism of the republic: all religious opinions have a common core which alone is worthwhile and true (and which is the concern of the republic as a whole), just as the development of every educational capacity, no matter how different, is essentially a part of a single human purpose — sustaining a common republican society. In the same way that religious groups have no identity for Jefferson (except as one kind of voluntary society founded by autonomous individuals), so also educational institutions have no independent identity. Schools are merely *functional* servants of *individual* growth and of *republican* virtue. With this view of people as autonomous individuals and of the republic as the only true and universal religious community of humanity, Jefferson felt no need to account for the distinct character of either educational institutions or churches.

Jefferson's educational plans reveal this fact conclusively. On the one hand his plans were designed simply to secure an education for every individual according to the capacity of each. On the other hand, his proposed organization of the schools was a completely political plan which assumed that one school system, under the majoritarian control of the body politic, could provide the uniform and common education that would satisfy every individual. From 1779, when Jefferson presented his first proposal for universal, public elementary education as a bill to the Virginia Assembly,[27] he was presupposing a political framework (geographical districts, public tax support, etc.) as the organizational framework and basis for education.[28]

Jefferson's writings occasionally reveal indications that he was aware of parental rights over children (even with respect to education)[29] and that he was aware of the fact that the church had traditionally exercised a great deal of control over education. But his universalistic republican attitude never allowed him to consider seriously either the church or the family as a legitimate authority in public education any more than it allowed him to consider the school itself as an institution with its own unique identity, distinct from the republic, the family, and the churches.

A most remarkable insight into Jefferson's understanding of the place of education in the republic comes from James B. Conant's search for the sources of Jefferson's educational views. Although Conant does not believe that his case can be proven beyond doubt, he nevertheless argues that the influence of Scottish Realism on Jefferson (through his teacher at William and Mary, William Small) brought with it the influence of the political structure of education in Scotland that went back to the ideas of John Knox in the Presbyterian Church's *Book of Discipline* of

1561.[30] Now clearly Jefferson was not sympathetic to Knox and Presbyterianism, but the structural identity and place of schools in Knox's plan for the Christian state served almost perfectly for Jefferson's plan for education in the American republic.

For Knox the church was the moral and religious director of the state. His plan for Scotland was to have a single Christian school system that would train good Christian citizens for the service of God in all areas of national life. From Conant's point of view Knox's plan was actually a scheme "to perpetuate a spiritual tyranny" in the state.[31] Conant believes that Jefferson took this idea of a single, politically organized system of education and transformed it into a scheme "to secure religious freedom and personal liberty in the new republic overseas."[32]

But how curious it is that Conant does not see the "spiritual tyranny" that is carried forward by Jefferson into the new republic. Of course, Jefferson's religious and moral principles for education were not identical with Knox's Calvinism. And it is also true that Jefferson desired to restrain government in a way that would leave individuals free outside the political order. But where is the freedom of individuals in Jefferson's scheme of education? One school system, run by the political community to train children in republican virtues (among other things), allows no more freedom to those who would desire another kind of education than did Knox's single school system to those who might have wanted something other than "Presbyterian education." Knox wanted to produce "conforming Christians" through the schools; Jefferson wanted to produce "conforming republicans" through the schools.[33] Since education was essential to the moral and rational development of an individual, in Jefferson's view, he was in essence arguing that individual freedom is dependent upon a uniform education within the republic.

Whatever can be said for Jefferson's confidence that all religions have a common core of moral truth that will sustain the republican commonwealth, it is clear he was entirely unwilling to leave the teaching of that common core to churches, families, and individuals. To the contrary, he believed that the power and authority of the people, organized in the several states of the universal republic, with majority rule, should be exercised to institute education as part of the very identity and meaning of the republic. The republic, in Jefferson's eyes, is, as we have shown, not a nonreligious, amoral mechanism. It is a truly universal, moral, and religious community. Thus, keeping John Knox in mind, we can argue, with Mead, that flowing directly from Jefferson's vision,

. . . the public schools in the United States took over one of the basic responsibilities that traditionally was always assumed by an established church. In this sense the public-school system of the United States *is* its established church. . . .

In this context one can understand why it is that the religion of many Americans is democracy—why their real faith is the "democratic faith"—the religion of the public schools.[34]

A further look at Jefferson's understanding of the function of public education substantiates our argument that the public school system in America becomes, in the Jeffersonian framework, the established church of the republic.

In an important letter to John Adams, October 28, 1813, Jefferson explained that his plan for education in Virginia was part of a larger program to replace an "artificial aristocracy" (including the clergy) by a natural one, and to do this by nurturing "equality of condition" among the people, raising them to that level where they would be able by their own power and good judgment "to select the able and good for the direction of their government.[35] Jefferson viewed the clergy as tyrants over the minds of the people, just as he viewed kings and wealthy aristocrats as tyrants over people's bodies and properties. What he desired was to throw down all tyrants, including clergy and other aristocrats, and to elevate the people to autonomous freedom. The means for accomplishing all of this would be free, public education.

But, of course, as we have seen, Jefferson recognized that not all individuals have the same capacity for education. What he actually anticipated was that the individuals with greatest capacity and talent for education would become the "natural aristocrats," the new republican leaders of the people. Whereas the clergy and the wealthy are unnatural, unacceptable tyrants, Jefferson believed that naturally gifted individuals who received a republican education would be nontyrannical and acceptable leaders. The mass of people would naturally choose and receive them as their leaders in politics, science, and education. Jefferson believed that a common republican education would thus not only guarantee the freedom of the mass of people so that they could be the best guardians of their own liberty, but would also guarantee the preparation of a group of "natural aristocrats" acceptable to the whole body of the people as their leaders. With one stroke Jefferson would knock out the false clergy and establish a new clergy—the republican priests of rational and moral autonomy.[36]

Again, however, we are brought back to the paradox of

Jefferson's attempt to secure individual liberty through a plan for uniform public education under the direction of a new elite. The individually free American would have to become the "perfectly homogeneous" American.[37] He would be "free" to sit at the feet of a new aristocracy to learn how to be free.

The underlying assumption of Jefferson's political universalism is that a people can constitute itself, through free association, as an integral homogeneous republic. His educational plan was designed to nurture that uniform peoplehood. Jefferson wanted a republican school system that "would produce homogeneous . . . political views."[38]

What are the consequences here for religious freedom and religious education? Jefferson's position can already be anticipated. Clearly, for him, all sectarian dogmas must be kept out of public education. The other side of the same coin is that any sectarian education is by definition nonpublic and not eligible for public support. Sectarian dogmas can only do more harm than good. There can be no public support for them (or for education sponsored by sectarians) because, by definition, people who are dependent upon dogmas are not free; special dogmas are not universal or common and therefore cannot be public. The dogmas of the sects and churches were, in Jefferson's eyes, abstractions and speculations of a "hyperphysical and antiphysical" character. They denied sense experience as the source and test of human knowledge and could only lead the mind "in to the fathomless abyss of dreams and phantasms."[39] Religious dogmas simply had no place in the training of individuals for autonomy and for republican homogeneity; they did not pass the rational test for acceptable public truth. They were heretical from a republican standpoint.

But Jefferson did not believe for a moment that education could be neutral with respect to the common essentials of religion and morality. The universal truths of morality and religion must be part of good education. For Jefferson the purpose of religion in public education is very simply that of aiding the moral development of youth.[40] As we saw earlier, however, the moral truths of religion are not so much intellectual ideas to be learned as they are moral convictions and habits to be practiced. Thus, religious training should help students to exercise their moral wills in order to develop good habits of doing what is right. By the time better students arrive at the higher levels of education they will be prepared to read supplementary works of the ancient Stoics and Epicureans and other moralists as well as the works of some seventeenth- and eighteenth-century empiricists.[41] Such reading will strengthen their minds with correct explanations of what their moral sense and wills had already habitually accepted. Finally, at the highest level of education students will be able to understand the empirically based proofs for God's existence, and then their religious education will be complete.

We should now be able to see how fully dogmatic, biased, and sectarian Jefferson's political philosophy and educational proposals really are. Although Jefferson believed that the true religion of republican morality is common and universal, it was actually but one "faith" among many. In his plan for public education, one "faith" and "moral system" would be established to the exclusion of all others. Nor was Jefferson entirely unconscious of this. In private letters he confessed his hope that the changes brought about by a public school system would include "a quiet euthanasia of the heresies of bigotry and fanaticism which have so long triumphed over human reason."[42] And by bringing the various sects together at the University of Virginia without allowing any single one to have a special position, he hoped that it would be possible to "liberalize and neutralize their prejudices, and make the general religion a religion of peace, reason, and morality."[43] But is this anything more than a restatement of Constantine's hope that a newly enforced public religion would be able to snuff out older enforced religions? Is this anything more than a plan to use political power for the support of a new faith in reason rather than for the support of an old faith in Christ?

Jefferson's plan did not really exclude dogmas from the public schools after all; it merely substituted the dogma of rationalistic empiricism and moralism for those dogmas belonging to the super-naturalistic revelation of Christianity. If doctrinal religion was to be studied at all, says Healey of Jefferson, "it was to be approached only from the point of view of strict dogmatic rationalism, and only by those whose fully matured reasons would give them the maximum possible invulnerability to sectarian doctrinal corruption."[44] Jefferson was bent on replacing an old religious conformity in society with a new one. The means was to be education.

Perhaps the best known illustration of Jefferson's sectarian dogmatism is found in his plan for the University of Virginia, where he insisted that an "orthodox" states' rights republican would have to be hired for the position of law professor and the texts would be prescribed for the field of government and not left to the decision of the professor. The study of government was the most important discipline for Jefferson, much as theology had been for the universities of the Middle Ages. In this field, he argued, it is our duty to guard against the dissemination of false doctrines (such as those of monarchists and federalists). Surely there is little difference at this point between Jefferson's plan and that of John Knox. As David Tyack explains:

> Jefferson's prescription of texts meant to a Federalist Virginian such as Chief Justice Marshall, who favored a strong central government, that he was being compelled by the state to contribute money for the propagation of opinions which he disbelieved and abhorred. If the true test of tolerance is to permit heresies about which one cares deeply, then the Virginian Federalists might appear greater libertarians than the man who "swore eternal hostility to tyranny over the minds of men."[45]

One of the most remarkable things about Jefferson's educational plan is that he was simply unfolding the implications of his political philosophy, which was itself the expression of his universalistic moral religion. In other words, unlike the different religious groups that were working with two religions, one public and one private, one natural and one supernatural, one rational and one pietistic, Jefferson was able at each step to unfold the integral wholeness of a single political/religious morality that embraced the totality of individual and republican life. In fact, the constitutions of Virginia and eventually of the United States embodied the Jeffersonian outlook so completely that he was able to develop plans for state-supported educational systems in which the legally permissible "common" morality and religion that would be taught were "just those areas in religion which Jefferson believed alone had a right to be in any worthwhile education, and the constitutionally offensive, sectarian tenets were just those religious areas which, Jefferson privately believed, endangered the human reason."[46]

OTHER ADVOCATES OF A NEW ORDER

Years before the founding of the republic and Jefferson's 1779 "Bill for the More General Diffusion of Knowledge," Benjamin Franklin had designed an academy to fire the minds of youth in his "Proposals Relating to the Education of Youth in Pennsylvania" (1749) and his "Idea of the English School, Sketch'd Out for the Consideration of the Trustees of the Philadelphia Academy" (1751). Franklin outlined a system of moral education designed to produce useful citizens.[47] Both proposals reflected Franklin's cosmopolitan, Enlightenment faith, which rejected both academic

custom and religious orthodoxy.[48] Franklin's concern for culti-
vating young minds was guided by his concern for republican
homogeneity. In the same year that he drafted his "Idea of the
English School," he wrote his friend James Parker to warn against
the increasing German threat to the colony. The significant German immigration into Pennsylvania after the 1720s was of peasant
origin and represented a striking contrast to the English in language, religion, values, and manner of life. While the provincial
assembly sought a number of ways to slow the German influx,
Franklin warned Parker that the immigrants were both a political
and cultural threat. A common English education was the only
answer.[49]

Benjamin Rush of Philadelphia, a close acquaintance of both
Jefferson and Franklin, was one of the first people after the Revolutionary War to address himself to the need for a system of
public education. By 1786, the year in which Rush published "A
Plan for the Establishment of Public Schools and the Diffusion of
Knowledge in Pennsylvania; to which are added, Thoughts upon
the Mode of Education, Proper in a Republic,"[50] it was obvious
to many Americans that new institutions, including a stronger
federal government, were needed if the republic was to survive.
Rush put his faith for the future republic in the development of
a public school system. For Pennsylvania this meant a university
established in the capital, four colleges located in different parts
of the state, college preparatory academies in each county, and
free schools in every township or in every district of one hundred
families.[51] "By this plan," Rush argued, "the whole state will be
tied together by one system of education." The result would be
that "the same system of grammar, oratory, and philosophy will
be taught in every part of the state, and the literary features of
Pennsylvania will thus designate one great and equally enlightened family."[52]

Rush, like Franklin, was quite conscious of the ethnic com-
plexity of the state, and it was in large part because of this awareness that he advocated a state-wide system of tax-supported public
education. "Our schools of learning," Rush predicted, "by producing one general and uniform system of education, will render
the mass of the people more homogeneous and thereby fit them
more easily for uniform and peaceable government."[53] In contrast
to Jefferson and some others, however, Rush accepted the public
presence of religious differences and supported denominational
education provided the schools championed republican values.[54]
He believed that Christianity is ideally suited to this because "all
its doctrines and precepts are calculated to promote the happiness

45

of society and the safety and well being of civil government."
According to Rush, "A Christian cannot fail of being a
republican."[55]

Although Rush was more willing than either Franklin or
Jefferson to identify himself as a Christian, his central loyalty was
to the republican state. It was the republican civil religion that
claimed his heart and led him to declare: "Our country includes
family, friends, and property, and should be preferred to them
all. Let our pupil be taught that he does not belong to himself, but
that he is public property. Let him be taught to love his family,
but let him be taught at the same time that he must forsake and
even forget them when the welfare of his country requires it."[56]
Rush's mind turned to the pagan histories of Greece and Rome
to find examples of such dedication, and he concluded that "the
history of the commonwealths of Greece and Rome show that
human nature, without the aids of Christianity, has attained these
degrees of perfection."[57]

There was little doubt in Rush's mind that a structure of
public education would make for a strong republic. He carefully
pointed out that "The principle of patriotism stands in need of the
reinforcement of *prejudice*, and it is well known that our strongest
prejudices in favor of our country are formed in the first one and
twenty years of our lives."[58] Rush unabashedly concluded: "From
the observations that have been made it is plain that I consider
it as possible to convert men into republican machines. This must
be done if we expect them to perform their parts properly in the
great machine of the government of the state."[59] "The wills of the
people," he argued, "must be fitted to each other by means of
education before they can be made to produce regularity and
unison in government."[60]

The phrase "republican machines" was well chosen by Rush,
since he envisioned public schools that would teach discipline and
respect for authority. The authority of the school, like that of the
family, was to be absolute, and yet no authoritarian structure was
to be an end in itself. The purpose of authority in school and
family was to "prepare our youth for the subordination of laws
and thereby qualify them for becoming good citizens of the
republic."[61]

Noah Webster shared Rush's belief that a system of public
education was the best way to ensure the survival of the republic.
Writing in 1780, Webster was also concerned that the republic's
"constitutions of civil government" were not yet firmly established
and the "national character . . . not yet formed."[62] The answer
to both challenges in Webster's mind was

. . . that systems of education should be adopted and pursued which may not only diffuse a knowledge of the sciences but may implant in the minds of the American youth the principles of virtue and of liberty and inspire them with just and liberal ideas of government and with an inviolable attachment to their own country.[63]

Webster's concern for the "American youth" was translated into a life-long effort to develop a common American language and curriculum for the schools. More than any other early supporter of public education, it was Webster who argued that foreign education should "be discountenanced, if not prohibited" and that the republic's honor as an independent nation should be nurtured directly through the establishment of literary institutions and books which would reflect republican values.[64] Since, according to Webster, the period between the ages of twelve and twenty was the most important in life for the shaping of personal and political loyalties, it was imperative that books "call home the minds of youth and fix them upon the interests of their own country." The principal schoolbook in the United States should include a "selection of essays respecting the settlement and geography of America, the history of the late Revolution and of the most remarkable characters and events that distinguished it, and a compendium of the principles of the federal and provincial governments."[65]

Although Webster opposed the use of the Bible as a schoolbook, he had no qualms about suggesting that a nationalistic schoolbook, as described above, ought to function as a nondenominational catechism in the public schools. The reason for this was quite simple. In the civil religion of Noah Webster, republican education had replaced the church as the chief integrator of public life. From his perspective,

Education, in a large measure, forms the moral characters of men, and morals are the basis of government. Education should therefore be the first care of a legislature. . . . A good system of education should be the first article in the code of political regulations.[66]

The need for a national system of education was one of the special concerns of the American Philosophical Society. Organized by Benjamin Franklin and others, the Society was responsible for encouraging trans-Atlantic discussions as well as creating a national consciousness by fostering dialogue among the colonies. When the Revolution had been won, the Society immediately set itself the task of advancing the purposes of the young republic. It was not surprising, therefore, that in 1797, the year Jefferson and Rush served as the two chief officers of the American Philosophical Society, it offered a prize for "the best system of liberal education and literary instruction, adapted to the genius of the Government of the United States; comprehending also a plan for instituting and conducting public schools in this country, on the principles of the most extensive utility."[67]

One of the essays that won the prize was written by Samuel Harrison Smith, who eventually became involved in politics as the editor of the *National Intelligencer*, the official newspaper of the Jefferson administration. Smith's essay is worthy of comment because of his straightforward assertion that education is the primary responsibility of the state. Having accepted Jefferson's republican ideology, Smith concludes that if public education is to be successful, "one principle must prevail. Society must establish the right to educate, and acknowledge the duty of having educated, all children. A circumstance so momentously important must not be left to the negligence of individuals."[68] Smith quotes approvingly the French lawyer Jean Jacques Regis de Cambacérès who argued, "It is proper to remind parents that their children belong to the state and that in their education they ought to conform to the rules which it prescribes."[69] In this approach to education there is little difference between Smith, the Jeffersonian, and Cambacérès, the Napoleonic statesman.[70] In their perspective the child, the family, and the school have meaning only within the structure and purpose of the state.

Although Jefferson, Rush, Webster, and Smith did not witness the desire of their hearts during their lifetimes, it was not long before a single system of compulsory, tax-supported, public education did emerge triumphant in America. And if we ask what forces culminated in the establishment of compulsory, free, public education, we can answer with Sidney Mead, "Must it not be said that prominent among the reasons was a desire to make possible and to guarantee the dissemination and inculcation among the embryo citizens of the beliefs essential to the existence and well-being of the democratic society?"[71]

EDUCATION AND THE ESTABLISHED CIVIL RELIGION

The main lines of argument can now be drawn together. Following other Enlightenment thinkers in their rejection of Christian faith and in their adoption of a rational moralism, Jefferson committed himself to a naturalistic, empirical quest for the common religion of universal morality. His presuppositions included both a trust in the self-sufficiency of empirical *reason*, which needs no aid from supernatural revelation, as well as faith in the testimony of *moral conscience*, which can provide the universal basis for social harmony and homogeneous community.

Jefferson's individualism did not extend to allowing individuals to act without respect to the common good simply on the basis of immediate feelings, intuitions, or convictions. In spite of the fact that he accepted the subjectivist implications of a *natural rights* doctrine that located *natural law* within autonomous individuals, his basic outlook remained that of a rationalistic universalist. It was not the diverse opinions, feelings, and ideas of individuals, in all their freedom and individuality, that had primary significance but the moral principles and rights which derived from the universal, rational order of nature. Jefferson's individualistic natural rights perspective was ultimately dominated by the universalism of his Enlightenment rationalism and moralism.

Due to the fact that theology and religion were traditionally identified with personal piety, with particular ecclesiastical establishments, and with unusual supernatural revelations, Jefferson believed that his antisupernaturalistic philosophy was nothing less than a universal, natural, rational, and undogmatic view of life that could be accepted by everyone solely on the basis of the self-evident testimony of the senses (including the moral sense). He remained relatively unconscious of the fact that his new faith was not less dogmatic than any other faith and that his religion of moralism was not a universal, self-evident religion among all people but one particular religion vying for dominance among others.

Given Jefferson's position, his fascinating political alliance with many Christians of his day is perhaps the most startling and amazing development of the late eighteenth century. The alliance produced much of our constitutional system as well as our system of public education. Jefferson's position was universalistic, envisioning only a single, homogeneous association (the republic) as the means for protecting individual freedom and nurturing social harmony. He was willing to accept a *limited* universal republic precisely because he believed in individual freedom outside and beyond the public association. But the intertwinement of the individual and the republic was so complete in his mind that, in fact, the individual was left with little else to be dependent upon socially beside the republic. The individual's rights to life, liberty, and happiness ultimately came to rest upon the power and stability of the republic to preserve them and upon republican education to nurture the capabilities of each individual so that he or she could truly enjoy them. Thus Jefferson was caught in a dialectic of "individual freedom" and "public order" that maintained a tension between anarchism on the one hand and totalitarianism on the other. This outlook was essentially monistic for Jefferson, however, because the dialectic was inherent in his presuppositions about the individual and the republic. His presuppositions were integrally bound together as a single rationalistic, naturalistic moralism.

Many Christians, on the other hand, accepted the *limited* though *universal* character of the Jeffersonian republic not because they accepted most of his presuppositions but because they were essentially dualists who made a non-Jeffersonian distinction between nature and supernature, between secular and sacred. For a large number of American Christians, Christianity was universal primarily (if not totally) in a supernatural, personal, spiritual, ecclesiastical reality that left the natural, secular world open to another universalistic organizing principle. Christians could accept Jefferson's universalistic republican principles because those principles appeared to be purely secular, *limited* to the public political realm, and not restrictive for personal piety and private ecclesiastical freedom outside the public realm. Not all Christians, to be sure, had given up the old ideal of a church-directed culture.[72] But large numbers of them were willing to accommodate themselves to a public order that would allow them to nurture and strengthen their Christian freedom. Jefferson, on the other hand, was primarily interested in the development and enlargement of a common public rationalism and moralism that would aid the "withering away" of strange, diverse, sectarian dogmas.

At the turn of the century, while the new American republic was just beginning to gain identity and strength, the Christian groups were prospering both in their churches and in a variety of unrelated educational ventures, many of them nonpublic. But by the mid-nineteenth century the Jeffersonian argument for a common public reasonableness and morality took hold at the foundation of a common public school system that threw government weight on the side of republican commonness rather than on the side of sectarian diversity.

In this we clearly recognize the establishment of a civil religion in America—an establishment that apparently flies in the face of the principle of religious freedom but which is in fact consistent with constitutional, Jeffersonian principles. "Religion" defined as private opinion, private voluntary associations (churches), and personal piety is, of course, not established politically and remains privately free. But "religion" in the Jeffersonian sense of a common religious morality that undergirds the social harmony of the republic has been established plainly and simply by the constitutional principles of the sovereignty of the people and the rule of the majority. That establishment has been furthered by a governmentally imposed public school system that monopolizes almost all public funds and legal support on the grounds that it is the only common, secular, nonsectarian school system and thus the only system capable of legitimately training *all* citizens for life in the universal republic.

Even if the particular Jeffersonian dogmas concerning God, humanity, and the world are now rejected by most Americans (and this does not assume that they are), the system of a single public school established to socialize children on the basis of what is common among the contemporary populace remains intact. That common, dominant framework may have been (may be) largely Protestant at one time and place, positivistic and rationalistic at another time and place, or something else at another time and place. But regardless of the content and direction of public education at any given moment in history, it is always guided by the Jeffersonian assumptions that a plurality of peoples or religious outlooks or philosophic perspectives does not and may not exist (except as personal piety and in private associations) in the homogeneous republic. Only one school system should be established (just as only one church was established in earlier centuries) to guarantee the social and moral homogeneity of the republic. American public education, founded upon Jeffersonian political principles, lies at the heart of the American civil religion.

CHAPTER 4

THE PUBLIC SCHOOL INSTITUTIONALIZED

THE EIGHTEENTH CENTURY

IN 1779 political liberals in Virginia supported a comprehensive set of democratic reforms designed to do away with the economic privilege of the landed aristocracy, to separate the church from the state, and to establish a system of public schools. The last two objectives took the form of Jefferson's "Bill for Religious Freedom" and "Bill for the More General Diffusion of Knowledge." In Jefferson's mind the two bills, introduced before the General Assembly, would help to establish a more democratic order for Virginia.[1] The companion bills demonstrate Jefferson's awareness that if the Anglican church were to be disestablished, then another institution had to be found (established) to provide for the common (moral) unity that he assumed was necessary for the preservation of society.

Jefferson's "Bill for Religious Freedom" passed the Virginia Assembly in 1786 by an overwhelming (74 to 20) majority. His effort to establish a system of public primary and secondary schools in Virginia, however, was not as successful.[2] The reasons are various and complex.

The Revolutionary War was fought in part to escape what the colonists perceived as the centralized authority of the crown and parliament. Opposition to the adoption of a federal constitution in the 1780s reflected the fear that many had of reestablishing a strong central government. Politically, therefore, any proposal for either a state-wide or national system of public education had to face the concerted opposition of politicians and citizens who rejected any attempt to usurp the powers of local authorities. Moreover, when the Constitution was finally adopted in 1789, the federal government was not granted the legal power to set up a national system of public education.[3] Thus, for those individuals who were committed to the principle that schooling is the responsibility of the church, local authorities, philanthropic agencies, or the parents themselves, there were powerful legal and political arguments at their disposal for opposing a centralized system.

In addition, the social realities of the late eighteenth century did not encourage widespread public demand for education. Most individuals were destined to enter trades in which there was little need for schooling beyond the elementary level. Even to the young men who were anticipating careers in the ministry, medicine, and law, the availability of apprenticeships lessened the need for extensive formal schooling. Not everyone agreed with Jefferson, Rush, or Webster that a system of public education was a desirable personal or societal goal. Thus many political, legal, and social realities combined to ensure the defeat of any plan for either a state-wide or a national system of public schools in the eighteenth century.

THE NINETEENTH CENTURY

The vision of public education was to be taken up, however, by the generation that came to maturity during the first decades of the nineteenth century. It was during this period that the original vision of the Revolutionary generation developed into the institution known as the public school. In order to understand the purpose and structure of the common school, it is important again to emphasize, along with Bernard Bailyn, that nineteenth-century public schools did *not* emerge from the mind of New England Puritans. Bailyn makes the point this way:

> The modern conception of public education, the very idea of a clean line of separation between "private" and "public," was unknown before the end of the eighteenth century. Its origins are part of a complex story, involving changes in the role of the state as well as in the general institutional character of society. It is elaborately woven into the fabric of early modern history.[4]

Before the emergence of a clean line of separation between private and public education, the established pattern for financial support for schools—whether in the middle colonies, the South, or New England—was the English practice of multiple sources. The actual colonial practice of school financing was usually a combination of private donations, student tuition, and, in some cases, public funding in the form of land grants and taxes. Schools receiving money from the government were considered "public" even though they were managed by private individuals or religious groups which acted, not as officers and agencies of the government, but as trustees responsible for the preservation of their institution's educational program and goals. The reason was simple enough: such schools were considered public schools because their education was providing a public service.

Only in the nineteenth century did public education become limited exclusively to nonsectarian, government-run and financed schools. The question that needs answering is whether this development was consistent with a just public order for a society that was increasingly pluralistic. To help answer this question it is necessary to review briefly the development of the common school as it came into existence in Massachusetts and New York City. These two examples clearly illustrate how a monopolistic educational model came to be established as the basis for all public education. Eventually this model spread through the rest of the United States.

MASSACHUSETTS

As we have already seen, Massachusetts had a long history of promoting an educated citizenry. Although there are many contrasts between the role and place of schools in the Bible commonwealth of the seventeenth century and the eighteenth-century republican Commonwealth of Massachusetts, the underlying concern for education remained the same. The 1780 Massachusetts constitution clearly stated that "the duty of legislators and magistrates, in all future periods of this Commonwealth, [is] to cherish the interests of literature and the sciences," and "to encourage private societies and public institutions" in the promotion of agriculture, sciences, commerce, the trades, and the arts.[5]

According to this constitution, both private societies and public institutions were to be encouraged in their educational enterprise. Private societies or academies played an important educational role in Massachusetts and in many other states in the late eighteenth and early nineteenth centuries.[6] The academy was organized as a corporate entity with its own board of trustees which hired a schoolmaster and teachers and raised funds for the institution. Michael Katz has labeled this model of public education "corporate voluntarism."[7] Because the academy's role in secondary education was widely recognized as serving a public interest, many states actively promoted its growth and development through grants of land and money. This was the case, as Katz points out, because in the early republican period " 'public' implied the performance of broad social functions and the service of a large, heterogeneous, nonexclusive clientele rather than control and ownership by the community or state."[8]

In this respect the practice of the Massachusetts legislature, beginning in 1797 and lasting well into the nineteenth century, of offering land grants to academies to promote their establishment in every county was similar to government support for academies in other areas of the country. The actual curricula, size, interests of promoters, location (urban/rural), and quality of the academies defy any generalization. However, in an effort to bring some order and to guarantee some standards, the common school movement developed in Massachusetts in the 1820s. Common schools, first elementary and later secondary, challenged and eventually replaced the academies as the dominant educational institutions of the state.

The common school movement, referred to by Katz as "incipient bureaucracy," attacked both the "corporate voluntarism" of the academies as well as the "democratic localism" of early community schools.[9] The structure of "democratic localism" was the district system in which each ward of a city or small town managed its own school. The district system emerged in the colonial era when it was assumed that an essentially homogeneous people could agree on basic religious and cultural values. The growth of an increasingly pluralistic society challenged the viability of this structure, because the rivalry between groups within most communities, city wards, or neighborhoods fostered political competition for control of the local school "in order to ensure the propagation of particular points of view, or, at least, the exclusion of rival ones."[10]

Leading figures such as Horace Mann and Henry Barnard attacked democratic localism for the reason that it permitted "51 per cent of the local parents to dictate the religious, moral, and political ideas taught to the children of the remainder."[11] One of the ironies of this criticism, however, is that the bureaucratic control of local schools at the state level, as envisioned by the reformers such as Mann and Barnard, presupposed the same majoritarian political principle. Under the common school plan it was possible for 51 per cent of voting adults (if not a small dictatorial, educational elite) to determine the religious, moral, and political ideas taught to everyone in the entire state, not just a local community.

The educational reform movement did not arise merely out of dissatisfaction with the traditional patterns of democratic localism or corporate voluntarism. It was part of a more general social reform movement that included such causes as the Sunday School, the temperance movement, and the antislavery crusades.

For many reformers, however, public education soon became what Horace Mann referred to as "a reform to end the need for reform."[12] The common school movement manifested the republican ideas of Jefferson, Rush, and Webster in the context of the urbanization, industrialization, immigration, and the democratization of politcs that characterized the era of Andrew Jackson.

One of the chief concerns of the common school reformers was to articulate and bring to bear the Enlightenment's messianic belief in nonsectarian public education for their own day. The public school movement did not develop in a vacuum—it was created by heirs of the Enlightenment. And what they created, as David Tyack has pointed out, was not "a 'private' school affected with the public interest, not a 'public' school supported in part by private charity—(but) a school controlled by publically elected or appointed officials, financed from the public treasury."[13] And, it should be added, this public system came to provide a state-wide, nonsectarian, though still largely Protestant education.

Horace Mann (1796–1859), the organizer and first secretary of the Massachusetts State Board of Education, was the preeminent apostle of religious nondenominationalism in the public schools. Strongly influenced by Unitarianism, Mann was concerned that the theological differences which divided the numerous sects should remain in the home and church, while in the public schools the "common" Christian beliefs should provide the basis for the child's moral and religious development. In his mind "the Religion of Heaven should be taught to children, while the creeds of men should be postponed until their Minds were sufficiently matured to weigh Evidence and Arguments."[14] This is in fact the familiar Jeffersonian distinction between religion as a common moral code and religion as a private promotion of sectarian dogmas and beliefs. Mann's "Religion of Heaven" referred to the nonsectarian ethical standards of Protestantism, while the "creeds of men" were the sectarianism which divided people into many and often hostile denominations. Mann's goal was to create, through the public schools, a homogeneous community based upon a common morality.

Although Mann was often discouraged, he never became disillusioned about his educational mission. After one relatively unsuccessful tour, he wrote that "when I am about to present my gospel of education in some new place, I feel as if I were standing in bad weather before the door of a house and vainly pulling the bell, with no one at home, or all too busy to see me."[15] But the zeal and eloquence of the evangelist calling people to support the "good news" of public education gradually moved the hearts and minds of a growing number of people. Mann was successful in appealing to the citizens of Massachusetts to vote liberal appropriations so that children might receive "the bread of life." Writing in *The Common School Journal* in February 1840, he declared:

> If I could go into your town meetings the coming March, and be permitted to plead this cause, I would entreat you by your love of country, by your love of man, by your love of those whom God has made dearer to you than life, to lift up your minds to the height and grandeur of this great interest, — the one object, I might almost say, for which you live. Open your hearts, I beseech you; open your hands, open your pockets. Make *large* appropriations, that you may pay instructors liberally for their work, and obtain such as are worth the pay.[16]

The need for good teachers and the development of a system of normal schools to train them was a concern not only of Mann but also of others like Daniel Webster and Edward Everett. Staunch Whigs, they were alarmed by such developments as the rapid increase in foreign immigration and the extension of the franchise during the 1830s and '40s. Their values and class bias led them to believe that the immigrants should become members of the democratic peoplehood, and one way to control and possibly convert them to a democratic way of life was through a system of state education.[17] The role of the good teacher was to inculcate "correct doctrine" lest the illiterate, poor, and foreign-born become a threat to the established institutions and way of life.

The issue of motivation is crucial to a proper interpretation of the educational reformers. We are not suggesting, as many radical historians do, that a "conspiracy of class or self interest" was the primary motivation of the nineteenth-century urban schoolmen and their supporters. For the most part the reformers sincerely believed that their culture, values, and religion were best for all people and thus should be the norm for all of society. The habit of overriding the rights of minorities became institutionalized, defended, and perpetuated, not so much as a planned "conspiracy" than as a consequence of the "imposition of majoritarian beliefs." The schoolmen and their supporters succeeded not because of a cunningly conceived strategy but because their Anglo-Saxon, Protestant, class commitments were shared by the majority of Americans. The power of the state was used by the majority to establish a way of life judged to be normative for every citizen.

There can be little doubt that urban schoolmen did create

educational systems, curricula, and pedagogical methods which reflected cultural and class assumptions. In fact the nineteenth-century public school became the mechanism charged with the responsibility of maintaining social order and cohesion and of instilling in children codes of conduct, social values, and occupational skills deemed desirable by a Protestant middle-class majority in an increasingly capitalistic/industrialized society. The imagined threat to the social and economic order represented by the poor, illiterate Irish immigrants is what led Horace Mann to argue that the best hope for the preservation of the existing system was state education. He believed that it was necessary to remove children from the evil influence of immigrant parents and to place them in the wholesome atmosphere of the school where the norms of upright and orderly social living could be inculcated. In asking for the moral and financial support of business leaders, Mann concluded:

> Finally, in regard to those who possess the largest shares in the stock of worldly goods, could there, in your opinion, be any police so vigilant and effective, for the protection of all the rights of person, property and character, as such a sound and comprehensive education and training as our system of common schools could be made to impart; and would not the payment of a sufficient tax to make such education and training universal, be the cheapest means of self-protection and insurance?[18]

Without doubt, then, public school education as "the cheapest means of self-protection and insurance" had social as well as class implications. If, as Katz argues, an attitude of inherent superiority of one group of people towards another is a sign of class or racist sentiment, then there is little question that many of the educational reformers were guilty of class bias or racism in their perception of immigrant children. To substantiate this charge one need only reflect on the words of the Boston School Committee as recorded in its Annual Report of 1845, where its task is described as being that of

> taking children at random from a great city, undisciplined, uninstructed, often with inveterate forwardness and obstinacy, and with the inherited stupidity of centuries of ignorant ancestors; forming them from animals into intellectual beings; and, so far as a school can do it, from intellectual beings into spiritual beings; giving to many their first appreciation of what is wise, what is true, what is lovely, and what is pure; and not merely their first impressions, but what may possibly be their only impressions.[19]

It was largely to deal with the menace of the urban poor, the illiterate sons and daughters of Irish Catholics who concentrated in particular wards of a city like Boston, that educational reformers devised a centralized school system which they could control.[20] The bastion of democratic localism, the district system, was replaced by a central board of education. Only in such a centralized system could the school become a wheel of social machinery in which children could be formed by the values of those who ran the machine. The next step would be to make schooling universal and compulsory.[21]

The success of educational innovators such as Mann was not assured at the outset. In the 1840s the proponents of democratic localism attempted to check the influence and as yet limited power of the Massachusetts Board of Education and the state's normal schools. A Committee on Education of the House of Representatives recommended in 1840 the abolition of both the Board of Education and the normal schools because of the danger of attempting to base all schools and teachers upon one perspective or model as was done in France and Prussia.[22] The House committee argued:

> Undoubtedly, common schools may be used as a potent means of engrafting into the minds of children, political, religious and moral opinions; — but, in a country like this, where such diversity of sentiments exists, especially upon theological subjects, and where morality is considered a part of religion and is, to some extent, modified by sectarian views, the difficulty and danger of attempting to introduce these subjects into our schools, according to one fixed and settled plan, to be decided by a Central Board, must be obvious. The right to mold the political, moral and religious opinions of his children, is a right exclusively and jealously reserved by our own laws to every parent; and for the government to attempt, directly or indirectly, as to these matters, to stand in the parent's place, is an undertaking of very questionable policy. Such an attempt cannot fail to excite a feeling of jealousy, with respect to our public schools the results of which could not but be disastrous.[23]

The House committee challenged the position of the educational reformers that public education could avoid feelings of jealousy by being neutral toward all perspectives. The committee pointed out that religion and politics so permeated all subjects that neutrality was never possible, and went on to argue that even if neutrality were possible it would not be desirable, because "A book, upon politics, morals, or religion, containing no party or sectarian views, will be likely to leave the mind in a state of doubt and skepticism, much more to be deplored than any party or sectarian bias."[24] In the end, however, the critics failed by a narrow margin to abolish either the Board of Education or its normal schools. Nevertheless, the Massachusetts House committee report is upheld, in part, by such twentieth-century educational historians as Katz, who concludes:

> Schoolmen who thought they were promoting a neutral and classless — indeed, a common — school education remained unwilling to perceive the extent of cultural bias inherent in their own writing and activity. However, the bias was central and not incidental to the standardization and administrative rationalization of public education. For, in the last analysis, the rejection of democratic localism rested only partly on its inefficiency and violation of parental prerogative. It stemmed equally from a gut fear of the cultural divisiveness inherent in the increasing religious and ethnic diversity of American life. Cultural homogenization played counterpoint to administrative rationality. Bureaucracy was intended to standardize far more than the conduct of public life.[25]

There is little question that there was a pressing need in Massachusetts and elsewhere for more educational opportunities for the countless numbers of urban children. Expanding educational opportunities for every person and upgrading professionalism, however, did not have to be synonymous with the establishment of government control over all public education. The fact that it was established is more a demonstration of the power of a majoritarian ideology than of the undisputed normativity of the structure.

NEW YORK CITY

The same majoritarian imposition that led to the establishment of a public school system in Massachusetts also occurred in New York City, although under somewhat different circumstances. Unlike Massachusetts, with its heritage of public support for schools, education in New York lacked community support until late in the eighteenth century.[26] In 1795 the state legislature appropriated $50,000 annually for five years as matching funds for towns which organized their own schools. Within a few years more than a thousand schools teaching almost 60,000 students dotted the state.[27] Encouraged by this development, the state legislature in 1805 set up a permanent school fund to support a public school system.[28]

For a time the educational history of New York City took a different course than the rest of the state. Rather than supporting district common schools as in upstate areas, moneys from the permanent school fund were used to support the city's existing church schools and the four charitable organizations that provided free education.[29] The allotment to both the denominational and charitable institutions was divided in proportion to the number of students given free education and was only to be used for teachers' salaries.[30] This system of subsidized educational pluralism was unique in the state, but it did not survive the growing pressure of the common school movement.[31]

What first emerged was an educational structure that Katz refers to as "paternalistic voluntarism."[32] In 1805 the New York state legislature granted a charter incorporating "The Society for establishing a Free-School in the city of New York, for the education of such Poor Children as do not belong to, or are not provided for by, any religious society."[33] The trustees, who included such notable citizens as DeWitt Clinton (then mayor of New York), recognized that neither the church affiliated schools nor the academies were meeting the needs of a growing number of children whose parents could not afford to send them to private schools and were not interested in having them educated by the parish schools conducted by Presbyterian, Episcopalian, Methodist, and Dutch Reformed congregations.[34] The trustees declared that their goal was to be "humble gleaners in the wide field of benevolence," touching only the unchurched poor, "such objects . . . as are left by those who have gone before."[35] The training of the urban poor was to be in the rudiments of literacy and in religion as the Society attempted "to counteract the disadvantages resulting from the situation [poverty and unreligion] of their parents."[36]

The New York Free School Society soon grew to the point at which its intention shifted; it now sought to be a reaper and not merely a gleaner in the educational harvest. The Society had very early received state aid to pay teachers' salaries, and in 1807 it alone was granted the "peculiar privilege" of receiving public funds to construct and equip its school buildings.[37] With this financial backing and the growing support of the community, the Society began to educate children without regard to the religious denominational affiliation of their parents. A large part of the Society's success was the result of its having convinced both individuals and religious groups that nonsectarian Protestant education could be thoroughly religious. As a result, most religious groups, except the Roman Catholics, Dutch Reformed, and Associate Reformed Presbyterians, relied increasingly upon the Society to educate the children of their poor families.[38]

The favored position of the New York Free School Society with respect to state funding continued until a serious controversy erupted in the 1820s.[39] The conflict revolved around a Baptist school, its aggressive recruitment of students many of whom were not Baptist, and a grant of state funds by the legislature to pay not only teachers' salaries but also construction and equipment costs.[40] The Free School Society was upset with this development because the loss of its "peculiar privilege" meant that it had to share building and equipment funds with other groups at a time of financial difficulty caused by the depression of 1819–1821.

The New York Free School Society's response was to argue that any reduction of state funds to its schools would destroy the common school system and replace it with a system of sectarian schools.[41] The Society did not so much attempt to defend its "peculiar privilege" as to attack the legitimacy of *any* public money going to support what it labeled "sectarian" education. Although the curricula of the Baptist and the Society's schools were substantially the same, the trustees of the latter argued that its religious instruction was nonsectarian and nondenominational. Virtually overnight the issue changed from the Baptist participation in public funding for building and equipment costs to the Society's argument that any public funding for sectarian schools was illegitimate. "It is totally incompatible with our republican institutions," the Society argued, "and a dangerous precedent" to allow any portion of the public money to be spent "by the clergy or church trustees for the support of sectarian education."[42]

The issue went before the New York secretary of state, who also served at this time as the superintendent of the common schools. While John Van Ness Yates supported the Baptist position by urging the New York legislature "to extend the 'peculiar privilege' to all denominations, to adopt uniform methods of tabulating enrollments, and to devise means to recover the value of any property secured with state funds and used for private purposes," his advice was not followed.[43] The legislature chose not to face the controversial issue and in November 1824 turned its authority to designate the city's recipients of school funds over to the New York City Common Council. The next year, on the advice of its legal committee, the council rejected the Baptist petition and ruled that no public money could thereafter go to "sectarian" schools.[44] Thus, the council accepted without further question the Society's definition of private/public schools and of sectarian/nonsectarian education.[45] As if to reinforce the claim that it alone represented nonsectarian, "public" education, the Free School Society changed its name to the New York Public School Society. Its property and buildings were turned over to the city, and the mayor and recorder were reappointed as ex officio members of its board.[46] The Society then received from the city a perpetual lease of the property and buildings as well as the legal recognition that only its Protestant, nonsectarian view of education would receive public support.[47]

The Society's nondenominational Protestantism had won the day and had attained the means for the propagation of the "common faith" of the majority. It is important to emphasize, as does Timothy L. Smith, that it was a nondenominational Protestantism which first established a majoritarian educational perspective and structure for the entire city of New York. Professor Smith concludes that "an evangelical consensus of faith and ethics had come so to dominate the national culture that a majority of Protestants were now willing to entrust the state with the task of educating children, confident that education would be 'religious' still."[48]

Thus an evangelical faith was established by Protestants as the educational perspective for the New York City public schools. But the idea of a majoritarian public structure was rooted in the religious assumptions of Jefferson and other Enlightenment figures. This comes through even more clearly in the conflict over the allocation of common school funds once Catholics began to challenge the Protestant majority and the New York Public School Society.

During New York City's early history the immigrant population was made up primarily of American-born white Protestants of Dutch or English descent. In 1800 New York was more than 95 percent Protestant divided into many denominations and sects. This comparatively homogeneous population remained stable until the early 1820s when large scale immigration of poor Irish began.[49] By 1830 the Irish of New York City comprised a significant ethnic community with its own newspapers, social clubs, professional elites, and schools.

The expanding presence and growing significance of Catholics challenged the Protestant majority in New York City. In 1831 the directors of a Roman Catholic orphan asylum pressed the Catholic claim for a proportional share of the public school fund before the common council.[50] The petition went before the board of aldermen, and after a great deal of debate, by the margin of one vote, the board decided to include the asylum in the list of schools entitled to receive public funds. It then sent the measure on to the board of assistants.[51]

Protestants and supporters of the Public School Society were outraged. The board of assistants was acutely conscious of the political pressure from all sides and on September 5 referred the whole question to a law committee to report on the constitutionality of the ordinance. The report of the committee was important not only for the fate of the Catholic claim but also as a clear indication of the future direction of the legal debate surrounding education.

The report concluded that Catholic schools were not entitled to public funds because they were not "common" schools. A common school was defined as one open to all in which "those branches of education, and those only, ought to be taught, which tend to prepare a child for the ordinary business of life."[52] The report continued by arguing that, "if religion be taught in a school, it strips it of one of the characteristics of a common school, as all *religious* and *sectarian* studies have a direct reference to a future state, and *are not necessary* to prepare a child for the mechanical or any other business."[53]

Such a moral judgment about the relevancy of religion to everyday life was itself clearly a religious judgment, though a judgment made on supposedly neutral, nonreligious, "secular" grounds. While a vast majority of Protestants in the city would *not* have agreed that religion was irrelevant to everyday life, they were content to support a supposedly neutral, nonreligious, "secular" argument if it meant that Catholics would be excluded from participating in the common school fund. Years later this legal argument would be championed by secularists who rejected traditional religion but who were nevertheless deeply religious in their secular world view. The origin of the secularist argument, however, dates from a time when defenders of orthodox Christianity were in the majority.

The duplicity of Protestants supporting a supposedly neutral, nonreligious, secular argument is highlighted by the declaration in the Law Committee's report that the schools of the Public School Society were legitimately common schools and thus had a just and legal claim to the school fund even though "a portion of the Scriptures is read in the morning by the teachers, without comment."[54] Actually, the Society's schools required far more than the reading of a portion of scripture without comment. In 1830 the board of trustees published a "manual" which was to be used by teachers in the primary departments at the beginning of school. The opening exercise for the youngest children contained in part the following recitation:

> *Teacher*. My dear children, the intention of this school is to teach you to be good and useful in this world, that you may be happy in the world to come. What is the intention of this school?
>
> *T*. We therefore first teach you to "remember your Creator in the days of your youth." What do we first teach you?
>
> *T*. It is our duty to teach you this, because we find it written in the Holy Bible. Why is it our duty to teach you this?
>
> *T*. The Holy Bible directs us to "train you in the way you should go."
>
> *T*. Therefore, my children, you must obey your parents.
>
> *Scholar*. I must obey my parents.
>
> *T*. You must obey your teachers.
>
> *S*. I must obey my teachers . . .
>
> *T*. God always sees you. *(Slowly, and in a soft tone.)*
>
> *S*. God always sees me.
>
> *T*. God hears all you say.
>
> *S*. God hears all I say.
>
> *T*. God knows all you do.
>
> *S*. God knows all I do. . . .
>
> *T*. May all you, dear children, learn, while attending this school, to be good and useful in this world.
>
> *S*. May we all, while attending this school, learn to be good and useful in this world.
>
> *T*. And, with God's blessing, may you be happy in the world to come.
>
> *S*. And, with God's blessing, may we be happy in the world to come.[55]

In light of this required "profession of faith" in the schools of the Public School Society, it is difficult to accept the Law Committee's finding that Catholic schools failed but the Society's schools passed a "secular" test for determining what constitutes a common school. The secular/religious distinction is only understandable as a self-serving definition used by Protestants with political power to exclude Catholics from participating in the common school fund.

Roman Catholics argued that the law committee's report established an unjust system of public funding for schools because "Jews, Christians of every denomination, deists, and unbelievers of every description, contribute their due portion to the school fund, and it ought to be so distributed and disposed so that all may participate in the benefits."[56] The Catholic argument continued:

It would be but a poor consolation to an individual to know that he may entertain whatever religious opinion he pleases, and attend any church he may select, and at the same time be legally compelled to contribute a portion of his property to the support of a school in which religious doctrines diametrically opposed to those he entertains are taught.[57]

Thus from the Catholic point of view the consolidation of the public school in the hands of Protestants who insisted upon the inculcation of their perspective in education was a violation of a minority's religious rights. They stressed that the very reading of scripture in school without comment was a sectarian Protestant practice. It was, therefore, impossible for them in good conscience to send their children to such institutions. But the law committee's report rejected this Catholic argument and set forth a basically secular/religious test as the norm for determining what qualified as a public school.

By the late 1830s the school issue became embroiled in the growing anti-Catholic agitation and the complex party struggles of New York politics. While the increasing numbers of Irish immigrants were welcomed as needed toilers in a growing industrial society, their presence aroused the nativist sentiments of that era's swelling American nationalism. The clannishness of the Irish, their habits, their poverty, and above all their intense religious loyalties to the Catholic Church were interpreted by nativists as a threat to an established way of life. The nativist movement in New York was mirrored in other parts of the country as immigrants experienced the plight of a minority in a majoritarian-minded society.[58]

In New York City the Democratic party attracted the bulk of the Irish vote,[59] while the beleaguered conservative and aristocratic Whig organization identified itself with the growing nativist movement. A group of young upstate Whigs, on the other hand, decided on a different course. For reasons of politics (to break the Irish-Democratic party coalition) and justice, Whigs led by William Henry Seward began championing the immigrant cause.[60]

As a result of the Panic of 1837 and divisions within the Democratic party the Whigs won the governorship in 1838. Encouraged by the victory, the party hoped to broaden its base of political support. In 1839 Seward, in his inaugural message as governor, responded to the needs of the vast number of immigrants. He was particularly concerned about the state's role in education, and one of the educational reforms he proposed dealt specifically with the plight of the German and Irish immigrants. There should be, he said, "schools in which their children shall enjoy advantages of education equal to our own, with free toleration of their peculiar creeds and instructions."[61]

In 1840, Governor Seward followed up this general statement with a more specific recommendation calling for "the establishment of schools in which they [immigrant children] may be instructed by teachers speaking the same language as themselves and professing the same faith."[62] The Catholics in New York City responded to the governor's message by pressing their long-standing claim to a proportional share of the common school fund. The cause was led by the newly appointed Bishop John Hughes.[63]

In a petition to the New York board of aldermen, Bishop Hughes argued that a monopoly of state funds for education was controlled by a private corporation which had as one of its goals the "early religious instruction" of children.[64] He went on to point out the obvious bias expressed toward Catholics in the "early religious instruction" and insisted that correction of the errors could not be possible *without giving just ground for exception to other denominations.*[65] In this argument Hughes clearly set forth the fundamental dilemma created by every effort to maintain a majoritarian, monopolistic public school system in a religiously pluralistic society. He pointed out that it was impossible for professing Christians to teach the "essentials of religion" without offending the conscience of some other Christians, because there would always be differences among Christians as to what the "essentials of religion" should be. And if it was assumed that religion could be completely dismissed from education, then students would be left "to the advantage of infidelity."[66] The fundamental dilemma of a majoritarian, monopolistic educational structure was plain. Since education would always be religious (never neutral) in some form, whether Protestant, Catholic, secular, or something else, a majoritarian system would always offend the religious conscience of those in the minority.

The Catholic opposition to the New York Public School Society reflected important cultural and class differences as well as differences of religion. Bishop Hughes charged that the cultural and class bias inherent in the Society's schools alienated the ethnic poor and their children. He pointed out that the Society had become so concerned with the increasing number of poor children who refused to attend school that it had appealed to the good ladies of New York to use the "persuasive eloquence of female kindness" to gain the confidence of the immigrants, and it had appealed to "the strong arm of the civil power" to make education compulsory.[67]

The Society offered education on the basis of the principles of Joseph Lancaster's system of mass education. Discipline was strict and competition keen in this system of monitored instruction which allowed one master to teach a number of older pupils, who, in turn, taught younger students carefully prescribed lessons.[68] Katz observes that this mechanistic form of pedagogy, which reduced education to drill, seemed appropriate to the directors of the Society "because the schools served lower-class children who could without offense be likened to unfinished products, needing to be inculcated with norms of docility, cleanliness, sobriety, and obedience."[69] The intended consequence of these pedagogical arrangements was that immigrant laborers should become "alert, obedient, and so thoroughly attuned to discipline through group sanctions that a minimum of policing would ensure the preservation of social order."[70] Such a system of education, Katz concludes, reflected the attempts of the New York Public School Society "to ensure social order through the socialization of the poor in cheap, mass schooling factories."[71] This was obvious to Bishop Hughes in 1840, and it was for this reason that he accused the New York Public School Society of cultural and class bias as well as religious discrimination against poor Catholic immigrants.[72]

The Public School Society and a group of Protestant clergymen replied that Hughes's charges were absurd. Pratt documents the fierce counterattack launched to depict the Catholic Church as a despotic monster and an un-American institution.[73] The press and city Whigs joined in the anti-Catholic crusade and attacked Governor Seward for his position on the school question. Democrats in turn used Whig attacks "to convince Irish voters that Seward was deceiving them, that he could not deliver on his school proposals because his party was not behind him."[74]

The proposed solution by the Catholics to the educational imposition of cultural, class, and religious values on their children would have returned New York City to its original practice of dividing the public school money proportionally among all the schools offering free education. The common council rejected this solution, arguing that such action would compromise the separation of church and state. While there was a willingness on the part of the council and the Public School Society to see changes in some of the most offensive passages in school textbooks, the assumption continued to reign supreme that nonsectarian religious education did not violate the civil or religious freedom of any patriotic American. Flagrant nativism, combined with religious/philosophical assumptions about the nature of religion, led many to reject the Catholic argument.

With the common council's sustained rejection of Catholic

demands for justice in education, Catholics decided to take their case before the state legislature. Although they were unsuccessful in getting funds for their schools, they were able to exert enough political pressure to convince politicans that some kind of solution to the issue had to be found.[75] The times were changing, and politicians, particularly Democrats (in true Jacksonian fashion), began attacking the New York Public School Society as a dangerous private monopoly over which the public had no direct control. The political debate resulted in a new school law which passed the legislature in 1842. The law allowed the Society to continue to operate its schools, but only as district public schools under the supervision of an elected board of education and state superintendent of common schools. In districts where a *majority* did not want to support the Society's schools, the people could establish new district schools supported by public funds.[76]

A crucial provision of the law prohibited the granting of public funds to any school in which "any religious sectarian doctrine or tenet shall be taught, inculcated, or practiced."[77] While Catholics thus failed to achieve their original demand for the incorporation of their schools into the public system, the law did break the city-wide monopolistic hold of the Public School Society. The structural consequences of this political development, however, meant little for the future of public education. In reality the only change, to use Katz's categories once again, was that the monopolistic structure of a paternalistic voluntary school system was transformed into a professional, bureaucratic, monopolistic structure of state government.

Catholics realized that the majoritarian, monopolistic structure would remain. Since they were in the minority, the only way for them to have schools which reflected their world view was to build and operate them at their own expense while continuing to pay taxes for the support of a majoritarian school system. Once Bishop Hughes became convinced that parents' and children's rights to a proportional share of the educational funds would not be realized, he decided to abandon public education and devote much of his remaining life to the building of a privately financed parochial school system in New York.[78] The Bishop was so convinced of the need for Catholic education that whenever he appointed a new pastor he insisted that the priest "proceed upon the principle that, in this age and this country, the school is before the church."[79] Vincent Lannie credits Hughes with being one of the first bishops to urge the development of a Catholic school system as an integral part of the American Catholic Church.[80] The bishop's educational vision was officially implemented by The

Third Plenary Council of Baltimore in 1884 which required every pastor to establish a school within two years and all Catholic parents to send their children to a Catholic school whenever one was available.[81]

An irony of the Protestant/Catholic educational struggle in New York is that in the end education for both Protestants and Catholics was defined by an essentially Jeffersonian-Enlightenment public-legal structure for schools. It must be emphasized that the victory did not come easily. But what eventually emerged was a majoritarian, monopolistic public school establishment that would have delighted Jefferson and his Enlightenment visionaries. Protestants paved the way for this development. In their effort to avoid allocation of public funds to Catholics they championed a nonpluralistic conceptual framework for education which satisfied their immediate political objectives and religious prejudices.

CONSEQUENCES OF THE STRUGGLE OVER SCHOOL FUNDING

It is important to make clear exactly what can be learned from the Massachusetts and New York school controversies and how these incidents relate to the arguments of this book. Educational historians have often used Massachusetts and New York as paradigm cases for the triumph of secularism in public education. Most often such works reflect less the actual historical situation than the authors' commitment that schooling *should* be secular, managed by professionals, and supported and funded by the state.[82]

Fortunately such biased historical interpretation has been corrected by recent scholarship. Timothy L. Smith, David Tyack, and others have demonstrated the significant nineteenth-century evangelical Protestant influence and control in the common school movement.[83] This was particularly the case in the new western communities where Protestant ministers were often the founders, teachers, and directors of the common schools.[84] Lyman Beecher's *Plea for the West* is a classic statement of missionary concern for schooling and a clear demonstration that schools and churches were allies in the quest to establish the kingdom of God in America. The continuing Protestant influence in the common school movement is thus important to keep in mind.

While there is the danger of wanting to conclude too much from the Massachusetts and New York school controversies, it is clear that the 1842 New York and 1855 Massachusetts laws prohibiting the granting of public funds to sectarian schools were extremely important. Both in Massachusetts and New York the variety of public educational structures which originally existed in the first half of the nineteenth century gave way to the common school movement, which in turn led to the governmental centralization and monopolization of all funding for public primary and secondary education.

In contrast to this development, England settled its religious/educational controversy in the 1840s by extending state grants to educational societies representing Wesleyans and Roman Catholics. Thus in England, while a monopolistic, Anglican ecclesiastical establishment continued, a system of subsidized pluralism emerged to support schools. This principle of multiple establishment was rejected in the United States during the eighteenth-century debate over multiple church/state establishment.[85] In the new republic all churches were disestablished, but they were replaced by monopolistic public school systems in the several states which tolerated other schools only if they paid their own way.

To be sure, this was a historical process that came slowly in some states and more rapidly in others. By the time of the Civil War five states — Wisconsin, Michigan, Indiana, Oregon, and Minnesota — had constitutional provisions against the use of public funds for sectarian purposes.[86] These constitutional provisions were in part a Protestant response to the school conflict in New York; the nativist reaction had indeed spread throughout the country.

Many of the western states that came into the Union after the Civil War also constitutionally prohibited religious instruction in public schools. This reflected a continuation of prewar nativist sentiments at the federal level. President Grant used the occasion of his annual message to Congress in 1875 to help gain nativist support for the Republican party. Grant proposed a constitutional amendment which would specifically prohibit any public funds for the direct or indirect aid of any religious sect and prohibit the teaching in public schools of any "religious, atheistic, or pagan tenets."[87] Grant's proposal led to a Republican drive in the House of Representatives to change the First Amendment of the Constitution.

The Republican national convention followed the lead of Grant and the Republican leadership in Congress. A specific plank in the Republican platform contended that

> The public school system of the several States is the bulwark of the American Republic; and with a view to its security and permanence, we recommend an amendment to the

Constitution of the United States forbidding the application of any public funds or property for the benefit of any school or institution under sectarian control.[88]

Although the Republicans were eventually successful in the 1876 presidential election, their desire for a constitutional amendment failed to achieve the necessary two-thirds support in the Senate. Congress was successful, however, in passing legislation which required all new states admitted to the Union after 1876 to adopt an irrevocable ordinance that not only guaranteed religious freedom but required the states to include provision "for the establishment and maintenance of systems of public schools, which shall be open to all the children of said States and free from sectarian control."[89] The legislation was applicable to North Dakota, South Dakota, Montana, and Washington. The same provision was contained in the Enabling Act of Utah, Oklahoma, New Mexico, and Arizona. The Idaho and Wyoming constitutions contained similar provisions.[90]

By the end of the nineteenth century the United States Congress had not yet provided funds for public education. It had determined through federal legislation, however, that specific states were required to establish and control nonsectarian public schools. In the twentieth century the federal government finally secured Jefferson's eighteenth-century vision of majoritarian public education in every state of the union. It did so by means of decisions of the Supreme Court.

CHAPTER 5

THE SUPREME COURT FACES THE SCHOOLS QUESTION

With the nineteenth-century establishment of the type of public school system that we have just described, the basic pattern for public education in the United States was set. Through the remainder of the nineteenth century and thus far in the twentieth, the history of education in America has been one of the spread and growth of publicly supported, bureaucratically centralized, and fiscally monopolistic school systems.

For many years, the various legal and political battles that were fought over education were contained for the most part at the local and state levels. Not until the 1930s and 1940s did the U.S. Supreme Court begin to address questions of educational freedom.[1] Today important legal struggles over the control of education almost invariably come before the Supreme Court. For this reason alone it is important that we take a close look at the Court's role in American education.

Our purpose, however, is a qualified one — qualified, that is, by the general argument and purpose of this book. We have no intention of writing a history of the Supreme Court's handling of education cases. We do not intend to analyze and criticize every relevant case. We have no interest in trying to distinquish "good" Justices from "bad" ones in order to berate the latter by means of the judgments of the former. Nor will we attempt to make conclusive judgments about the significance and influence of the Court as compared with other agencies of government or other institutions in society. Furthermore we would like to be able to avoid both overestimating and underestimating the Supreme Court as an instrument of either progressive change or conservatism in regard to the future of education in America.

What we do want to achieve by an examination of the Supreme Court is a clarification of the manner in which it has been confronting the dilemmas and difficulties of our peculiar American establishment of education. The Court does not stand outside the "American way of life," even though it is often called upon to settle certain legal disputes at the highest level—the last court of appeal. Our primary question is this: Has the court gotten to the bottom of the fundamental problems facing us, and is it helping to clarify and resolve those problems in a proper, legal fashion? Or is it continuing to make its decisions in the context of dilemmas and ambiguities that it can neither see through nor resolve?

JUDICIAL REASONING

The Justices of the Supreme Court do not have the general task of philosophers or political theorists. Nor have they been assigned the task of making general scientific or historical judgments of an academic sort. And clearly their responsibility is not, first of all, either to educate the public or to draw up public policy options for the legislative and executive branches of the government. Rather, the Court, standing at the pinnacle of the judicial system as one of the three branches of the federal government, has a legal or juridical responsibility that must guide and qualify its mode of reasoning. Thus, as Dennis Thompson argues, the "judicial reasoning" of the Court should aim at persuading by means of judicial soundness without propagandistic manipulation.[2]

Our examination of the Supreme Court's arguments in the school cases, then, should seek to elucidate the Court's assumptions about, and guiding principles for establishing, "judicial soundness." To the extent that the Court has been persuasive in its reasoning, we should try to understand why that has been possible; at the same time we should ask about the reasons for its lack of persuasiveness to the extent that it has failed to convince its audience of "judicial soundness." The point of Thompson's article, in this respect, is to explain why he believes that the Court's reasoning in one particular case (*Abington School District* v. *Schempp*, 1963) was superior to that in three others (*Engel* v. *Vitale*, 1962; *Everson* v. *Board of Education*, 1947; *McCollum* v. *Board of Education*, 1948).[3] For instance, in *Everson* and *Engel*, says Thompson, Justices Rutledge and Black attempted to establish the original meaning of the First Amendment to their own satisfaction; and having done so, they rested their case. But even if we assume that there is an unambiguous, original meaning of that amendment (which is not generally granted), the question still remains how that meaning is relevant to our situation today. The Justices simply failed to produce an adequate historical argument to explain the relevancy of these cases. History, in other words, was not used to persuade us of the judicial soundness of the Court's decision.

Mark DeWolfe Howe provides a similar illustration. Howe examines Justice Frankfurter's appeal at one point to "social custom." In *McCollum* Frankfurter insisted

> that a social and not a legal commitment to the separation of church and state throughout the nation had been made before the adoption of the Fourteenth Amendment. "Separation in the field of education . . . was not imposed upon unwilling States by force of superior law. In this respect the Fourteenth Amendment merely reflected a principle then dominant in our national life."[5]

But is a dominant social commitment a sufficient basis for the Supreme Court's constitutional judgments?

These two examples alone raise the following questions: How should the Court think and reason correctly about the relation of constitutional law to history and society? Should something be judged legal and constitutional by the Court merely because a large portion of society has come to accept it? Should the Court perhaps have avoided civil rights decisions favoring blacks twenty-five years ago because the majority of whites were not yet ready to accept the principle behind those decisions? How does the legal protection of social minorities (religious as well as racial) fit into a constitutional system that gets its main direction through majoritarian will and control? How should the Court handle new historical situations that were not anticipated by the original Constitution and for which no new amendments have been made—situations such as the growth of a massive public school system?

Clearly, judicial reasoning which aims to persuade its audience of its own soundness is not an easily defined technical process. To the contrary, the interpretation of constitutional law is as complex as the political and social systems that the Constitution is supposed to define and uphold.

THE SOCIAL-HISTORICAL CONTEXT OF JUDICIAL REASONING

Precisely at this point the significance of the historical and philosophical discussions in earlier chapters becomes apparent, because the context or framework for judicial reasoning today has been established by the historical events, social structures, and deep convictions of the past two centuries. This is not to say that the course the Court follows is predetermined either by what has happened or by what now exists. The Court ought to face the problems and tensions and ambiguities of today with critical acumen and creative vision. But we should not be surprised to find that the Justices of the Supreme Court, as they try to act in a socially and historically responsible fashion, reflect the context in which they are rooted. And they do so to an extent that often does not allow them to produce judgments that penetrate and illuminate a given situation from a standpoint beyond the situation itself.

The preceding chapters describe some basic elements that form the structure of contemporary American society. We argued, for example, that by the end of the nineteenth century a firm commitment to the separation of church and state was built upon the common view that religion is connected with the churches and with personal faith, and that the state is a neutral, secular, and common body. Religious freedom came to be identified primarily with freedom of personal conviction and freedom of ecclesiastical association. The neutrality and secularity of local, state, and federal governments, on the other hand, meant that churches and private convictions were to be neither hindered nor specially aided by governmental institutions, and that government should serve only the common, secular interest as defined by some kind of majoritarian consensus. Schooling emerged, however, with an ambiguous identity as both a publicly supported, common, neutral, secular institution (as a function of the republic) and as a function of personal and parental responsibility that expresses itself in the nurturing of children to maturity—a maturity of personal faith and morality, individual freedom, personal responsibility, and in many cases, nonpublic vocations.

Religion itself shared in the ambiguity of identity that marked the schools. From before the time of Jefferson, but especially after Jefferson, the very meaning of religion was characterized by a fundamental ambiguity. By the second half of the nineteenth century (though it was not so obvious then), Sidney Mead explains,

> the United States, in effect, had two religions, or at least two different forms of the same religion, and . . . the prevailing Protestant ideology represented a syncretistic mingling of the two. The first was the religion of the denominations, which was commonly articulated in the terms of scholastic Protestant orthodoxy and almost universally practiced in terms of the experimental religion of pietistic revivalism.
> The second was the religion of the democratic society

and nation. This was rooted in the rationalism of the Enlightenment (to go no farther back) and was articulated in terms of the destiny of America, under God, to be fulfilled by perfecting the democratic way of life for the example and betterment of all mankind.[6]

This syncretistic or dualistic Protestantism worked its way out in the nineteenth century in a way that gave most Protestants some sense of both religious wholeness (after all, governments and schools were staffed, for the most part, by WASPs) as well as a sense of being dedicated to religious freedom for others and to a common, "neutral" republic. But Roman Catholics did not have the same experiences as Protestants. Catholics certainly gained "religious freedom" in the sense that their churches had freedom to exist, along with other "sects," in private. But one thing was quite clear, as Elwyn A. Smith puts it: "Catholicism was no part of the recognized religion of the country."[7]

Part of what we will seek to demonstrate in the following pages is that the ambiguous religious/secular framework that has functioned since the nineteenth century as the accepted ideology for defining relationships among states, churches, families, and schools remains the framework for judicial reasoning in the Supreme Court today. And because of the problems inherent in that framework, the Court has not been able to demonstrate "judicial soundness" in its interpretations. Stephen Arons explains:

> Up to this point, the effect of the Court's schooling cases has been to uphold and entrench the legal fiction that schooling can be value-neutral. By its use of the secular-religious dichotomy the Court has been able to eliminate an obvious form of belief manipulation — religious observance — from public schools, but it has thereby implied that the secular content of schooling does not touch upon the basic beliefs and values of students or that such secular values are unworthy of protection.[8]

Another way of putting it is that the so-called secular values which the Court does want to allow and protect in public schools are those of the majoritarian consensus. The Court believes those values to be essential for the health of the republic even if they offend the convictions of certain minorities.

The debate over secular and religious values, which soon broadens into the debate over majority and minority rights with respect to religious freedom, also reveals several of the basic structural problems of the public order that will concern us. And here again the Court shares in a general consensus among the

American people. A large majority of Americans grant that a single public school system ought to exist and ought to be controlled by means of majoritarian political institutions. Arons comments: "In almost all the struggles over the content, structure, and methods of public schools, the underlying agreement among the combatants has been that majoritarian political control of the school system is appropriate."[9]

Several of these basic political/legal assumptions have been accepted with so little critical reflection that the Court as well as all "combatants" continue to work with them unquestioningly in spite of their problematic ambiguity. Majoritarian political control of a single public school system is just one of those assumptions. The religious/secular dichotomy is another. Yet another is the conviction that diversity is healthy in private but unhealthy in the public arena. And a fourth implication is the continued willingness to live with an inadequate constitutional identity for certain institutions, such as families and schools.

SUPREME COURT STANDARDS, CRITERIA, AND TESTS

All these problems and ambiguities are apparent in the Supreme Court's legal standards and tests. In struggling to deal with the issue, the Court has developed three separate standards to guide judicial decisions regarding schools and the establishment clause of the First Amendment. They are outlined by Dennis Thompson.
1. Beginning with *Everson* (1947) and continuing in *McCollum* (1948), Justice Black articulated the standard of "absolute separation" of church and state for disallowing any state aid to religious schools. The doctrine behind this standard is still held firmly by many legal, educational, and religious authorities today, though the Supreme Court has moved away from it in recent years.[10] This standard gains its force and legal stature from the general consensus about the separation of religion and the state that goes back to Jefferson and Madison.[11] Since the state should do nothing to aid sectarian religion, it should be prohibited from giving any aid to nonpublic, religious institutions, including schools. In *Everson* the court did nevertheless allow New Jersey to reimburse parents of nonpublic school children for the costs of busing their children to school. The reason for the decision, however, reinforced the standard of absolute separation, since it maintained that such aid has a neutral, "public purpose," "child benefit" character that does not directly support any religious establishment.[12]

The judicial soundness of this decision depends on two suppositions. First it assumes that the religious/secular dichotomy pertains to schools clearly and unambiguously. Second, it assumes that there is no problem in distinguishing between a "secular" benefit to the individual child on the one hand and the context within which that benefit is bestowed on the other. The problem of the religious/secular distinction carries over to the "child benefit" principle. The child, who is obviously a citizen of the state, also happens to be, at the same time, a member of his or her family and a student at a "religious" school. Any benefit to the child also accrues to the religion of the child's family and school. Without clarifying the meaning of religion or defining the proper relationship of the state to schools and families, the Court only adds to the confusion by implying (without demonstration) that indirect aid to a child's private education by way of reimbursing the parents for transportation is *not* aid to religious schools. Absolute separationists were not persuaded by Black's reasoning, because they could make the argument that any support to parents (who pay the tuition) is an aid to private religious education.[13] Moreover, as Thompson and Smith both point out, the standard of absolute separation does not begin to do justice to the "free exercise" clause of the same amendment. It is clearly unconvincing judicial reasoning to those who are genuinely concerned about "free exercise" as a constitutional principle.[14]

2. The fact that not everyone in the court's audience was convinced of the judicial soundness of its reasoning on the basis of the "absolute separation" principle led Justice Douglas, for one, to attempt the definition of another standard in Zorach v. Clauson, 343 U.S. 306 (1952). Thompson calls this the standard of "cooperation" which was supposed to allow religious institutions and government the right to cooperate as long as direct support of religion by the state was either avoided or kept to a cautious minimum. Whereas in *McCollum* the Supreme Court had declared unconstitutional the right of public schools to allow religious education *within* the schools on a "released time" basis, in *Zorach* the Court upheld the right of public schools to grant students "released time" for religious education *off campus*.

Clearly Douglas was trying to take seriously the fact that the "free exercise" of religion is a constitutional right for citizens; to enforce strict separationism would conflict with that right. Wilbur G. Katz points out that the *Zorach* decision makes the "separation of church and state" dependent on the overriding principle of "religious liberty." Thus *Zorach* "may be read as holding that aid to religion is a proper legislative purpose so long as the aid involved is relatively minor."[15]

But does the "cooperationist" standard overcome the problems in distinguishing religion from secular neutrality? Does it provide a convincing definition of what constitutes minimum cooperation, a cooperation that avoids excessive entanglement of the state in religion while truly promoting religious liberty? To the contrary, Douglas's argument in the end is no more convincing than Black's "separationist" argument, even though it appeals to the general consensus about religious liberty in the context of a secular state.

3. A third standard the Court has proposed for dealing with school cases is that which Thompson labels "neutrality." According to this principle, the Court should require that the government be neutral in religious matters. But, says Thompson, at least four different conceptions of neutrality have been applied at different times, and three of them he finds so problematic as to be unacceptable.[16]

The standard for neutrality that Thompson finds acceptable is what he calls "wholesome neutrality." The Court began to enunciate this version of the neutrality principle in the *Schempp* decision of 1963. "The standard the Court now asserts," according to Thompson, "is that if the 'advancement or inhibition' of religion is the 'primary' legislative 'purpose' or 'effect' of a law, it violates the Establishment Clause."[17] If laws can be passed that do not have such a primary purpose or effect, they are legitimate. Nevertheless, the Court has yet to resolve two problems, says Thompson. First, there is the lack of clarity about what "primary purpose and effect" means. And second, there is the question of the applicability of this standard to other situations that may be unlike the *Schempp* case.[18]

But there is a further problem with this idea of "wholesome neutrality" that Thompson does not recognize. Thompson as well as the Supreme Court Justices focus their attention on laws that assume the present political-educational structure of public and private schools. They have not yet questioned the legitimacy of that structure itself. If it turns out, however, that the very existence of the present system of public education alongside independently financed private schools is religiously discriminatory both by inhibiting free exercise and by sustaining an illegitimate establishment, then all of the efforts to find subtle ways to remain "neutral" within the present system are in vain.

In *Schempp* the Court ruled that Pennsylvania's required Bible reading in the public schools violated the establishment clause of the First Amendment. Perhaps the key sentences in the majority opinion written by Justice Clark are the following:

> The place of religion in our society is an exalted one, achieved through a long tradition of reliance on the home, the church and the inviolable citadel of the individual heart and mind. We have come to recognize through bitter experience that *it is not within the power of government to invade that citadel, whether its purpose or effect be to aid or oppose, to advance or retard. In the relationship between man and religion, the state is firmly committed to a position of neutrality.*[19]

Clark's words display all the problematic implications and assumptions that we have discussed in the foregoing pages. First, he assumes that religion is something unambiguous, having its identity clearly *outside* the state, when in fact that has not been demonstrated to be the case. Second, because of this preconception about religion, Justice Clark overlooks one of the central institutions in our society that has promulgated our exalted religious traditions, namely, the *schools*. He refers only to the home, the church, and the individual as the great centers of religion. But that reference is simply the standard dogma passed on by our habit of thinking in terms of the religious/secular, public/private dichotomies. In fact nongovernment schools were the centers of Christian training for decades into the nineteenth century, and even by the end of the nineteenth century, Protestantism, both in its pietistic as well as in its republican religiosity, thoroughly penetrated the so-called nonsectarian, public schools. Clark and his colleagues have simply not come to grips with the actual history and real identity of the school in America.

Moreover Clark assumes that the government can in fact be neutral toward the citadel of the human heart and mind while it controls and finances the public school system. But the establishment of one monopolistic public school system, controlled by local and state majoritarian political institutions, is not and never has been a neutral secular establishment. It was not neutral as Jefferson and others conceived it; it was not neutral when it was controlled by the Protestants; it was not neutral when the Bible was required for devotional reading; and it is not neutral now that individual children are "protected" from hearing the Bible being read. The question is not whether neutrality can be maintained by reading or not reading the Bible in the public school, but whether a single monopolistic public school system can guarantee neutrality.

There is one slight hint in *Schempp*, found in Justice Stewart's dissenting opinion, that the crucial problems have not been totally ignored. Stewart remarks that

> a compulsory state educational system so structures a child's life that if religious exercises are held to be impermissible activity in schools, religion is placed at an artificial and state-created disadvantage. Viewed in this light, permission of such exercises for those who want them is necessary if the schools are truly to be neutral in the matter of religion. And a refusal to permit religious exercises thus is seen, not as the realization of state neutrality, but rather as the establishment of a religion of secularism, or at the least, as government support of the beliefs of those who think that religious exercises should be conducted in private.[20]

Stewart goes much nearer the heart of the matter than Clark in that he recognizes the religious (or at least nonneutral) character of political decisions about the schools. If one kind of "religious exercise" is forced out of the school, it is due to the imposed conviction of secularism. The Enlightenment bias against Christianity, therefore, is not neutral, but is a new form of established religion. However, the way in which Stewart phrases his dissent shows that he is not really calling into question the political *structure* for public education. He still assumes that religion is a separable activity that occurs alongside other nonreligious educational activities. Whether he is trying to identify an imposed "religion of secularism" or some other imposed religion, he has started with the assumption that the government-supported public school system, as a secular institution, can find a way to be neutral to all religions within it. But the question at the deepest level is whether the Enlightenment republican assumptions about "religion" and the "neutral secular republic" do not themselves violate the free exercise of religion and the nonestablishment of religion by their very imposition of a majoritarian, monopolistic political structure on education.

The Court handed down another important decision in Lemon et al. v. Kurtzman, 403 U.S. 602 (1971; hereafter referred to as *Lemon I.*) In this decision the Court's majority decided that Pennsylvania had gone too far in attempting to aid the "secular" aspects of "religious" schools and had actually become entangled in aid to religion. Justice White alone dissented, being convinced that the state was not excessively entangled in religion in this case. Once again, the crucial questions about what constitutes the "religious" and the "secular," and about what a school is in relation to families, the state, and the churches, were not asked or answered. Chief Justice Burger's opinion for the majority is another clear manifestation of the Court's bondage to the ambiguities and dilemmas of the American Enlightenment ideology.

Burger admits that the religion clauses of the First Amendment are "at best opaque." But without being able to explain what makes them so opaque, he is content to summarize the three criteria which the Court has gradually developed over the years to guide it in use of the "neutrality" principle.

> Every analysis in this area must begin with consideration of the cumulative criteria developed by the Court over many years. Three such tests may be gleaned from our cases. First, the statute must have a secular legislative purpose; second, its principal or primary effect must be one that neither advances nor inhibits religion, Board of Education v. Allen, 392 U.S. 236, 243 (1968); finally, the statute must not foster "an excessive government entanglement with religion."[21]

Burger grants Pennsylvania (and also Rhode Island in a related case) the legitimacy of the distinction between the secular and the religious in education. And he also admits that the "absolute separation" dogma is no longer adequate to handle this religious/secular distinction: ". . . total separation is not possible in an absolute sense. Some relationship between government and religious organizations is inevitable."[22] A proper relationship between two aspects of life that are supposed to be kept separate, therefore, will have to be built on the basis of the assumed purity of the state's secularity with its aid given only to the purely secular aspects of the "religious" schools.

> Our decisions from *Everson* to *Allen* have permitted the States to provide church-related schools with secular, neutral, or nonideological services, facilities, or materials. Bus transportation, school lunches, public health services, and secular textbooks supplied in common to all students were not thought to offend the Establishment Clause.[23]

The fact that in his argument the Chief Justice can abstract books, lunches, health service, and buses from the school, as though these things are not part of the educational institution's single integral identity and purpose, can only be explained in terms of his prior commitment to the religious/secular dichotomy in terms of which he wants to reduce all social facts to two categories: religious or secular. But a school, or a state, or a family, or any other institution is a social whole that cannot be cut in two pieces.[24]

Not only does Burger fail to recognize the identity of the

school as an integral institution distinguishable from churches and states, but his continued reliance upon the religious/secular dichotomy simply leads him to reiterate the old Jeffersonian confession of faith about the morally unified, nonsectarian, universal republic as the meaningful root and source of his judicial reasoning. He concludes, in other words, not with a new and better line of judicial argument, but simply by referring old arguments back to the religious root which gives them meaning, thereby appealing to his audience to confess with him the old faith. But the old Enlightenment faith is not held by everyone in the republic; some of these school cases are in fact calling that very faith into question. To reiterate the old confession of faith is not to present a sound judicial argument; it only reaffirms the faith of those who already believe, while closing off the most important avenue toward resolving serious problems of injustice in education.

Burger's approach along these lines is best illustrated by his appeal to the "whole history and tradition" of America for the purpose of warning us of the "divisive political potential" of the Pennsylvania aid program. If more and more public money goes to aid private schools, says Burger, the country might face increasing political division along religious lines. And whereas ordinary secular political debates and divisions are part of the healthy democratic process, in Burger's mind, he believes that it is not healthy to have political partisanship along religious lines.

> To have States or communities divide on the issues presented by state aid to parochial schools would tend to confuse and obscure other issues of great urgency. We have an expanding array of vexing issues, local and national, domestic and international, to debate and divide on. It conflicts with our whole history and tradition to permit questions of the Religion Clauses to assume such importance in our legislatures and in our elections that they could divert our attention from the myriad issues and problems that confront every level of government.[25]

What Burger is actually doing here is adding a fourth test for constitutionality to the three which he enumerated earlier. This fourth test determines whether a particular law aiding private education will lead to social friction or political division. If it would seem to do so, it is dangerous and therefore a threat to the national moral security. But we must ask the Chief Justice why, in his scale of relative crises, the relation of the religion clauses to education is so less urgent for the republic than other issues and problems that confront the government? His answer comes in the repetition of another old confessional formula: "The Constitution decrees that religion must be a private matter for the individual, the family, and the institutions of private choice, and while some involvement and entanglement are inevitable, lines must be drawn."[26] Not only is it the case that the Constitution decrees no such thing about the private character of religion but also it is clear that Burger is merely repeating certain contradictory clichés without clarifying the proper relation of the states and the churches to educational institutions. To say in one breath that religion must be exercised in private, and that entanglement between religion and government is inevitable, and that lines must be drawn, is to put phrases together that have no consistent logical, legal, or linguistic meaning except as a confession of a dogmatic faith that the Justice will neither let go nor examine.

In *Lemon I*, the only flicker of light that exposes the problematic confusion of the Court comes in Justice Douglas's opinion — an opinion which nevertheless supports the majority. According to Justice Douglas:

> While the evolution of the public school system in this country marked an escape from denominational control and was therefore admirable as seen through the eyes of those who think like Madison and Jefferson, it had disadvantages. The main one is that a state system may attempt to mold all students alike according to the views of the dominant group and to discourage the emergence of individual idiosyncrasies.[27]

But Douglas's vision is limited here to the problem of individual freedom within the public school system, and he does not go on to suggest any alternative that the Court or the states might suggest to different groups seeking real freedom and justice in education.

A year later in Wisconsin v. Yoder, 406 U.S. 205 (1972), the Court handed down an extremely significant decision that we will consider in slightly more detail below. For now, we should note that it was the first Supreme Court decision to grant partial immunity from compulsory school attendance requirements to a religious group, in this case an Amish group in Wisconsin. The decision, in other words, was based on the free exercise clause of the First Amendment, and it recognized an important limit to state monopoly over education.

But even in this case the reasoning of Chief Justice Burger, who delivered the majority opinion, followed well-established lines determined by the prevailing ideology. In evaluating the claims of the Amish, said Burger, we must be careful to determine whether their "religious faith and their mode of life are, as they claim, inseparable and interdependent." This is important, according to Burger, who believes that life can be separated from faith, because

> A way of life, however virtuous and admirable, may not be interposed as a barrier to reasonable state regulation of education if it is based on purely secular considerations; to have the protection of the Religion Clauses, the claims must be rooted in religious belief.[28]

Burger's assumptions here are clear. First, religion is so separable and distinguishable from life that it is possible to differentiate a life guided by religion from a life guided by purely "secular considerations." The fact that a year earlier the Chief Justice stated that the religion clauses are "at best opaque" does not keep him from holding firmly to the idea that religion can be clearly distinguished from secularity or irreligion. Moreover, the Chief Justice assumes that the First Amendment defines religion in a way that is sufficient to keep it from protecting irreligious or nonreligious persons. And third, Justice Burger is convinced that if the distinguishable religious factor cannot be appealed to by nonreligious people, then they have no ground whatever for escaping the majoritarian educational requirements that are imposed on all citizens no matter how different and virtuous and admirable may be the education they might prefer to give to their children.

The very concept of ordered liberty, according to the Chief Justice,

> precludes allowing every person to make his own standards on matters of conduct in which society as a whole has important interests. Thus, if the Amish asserted their claims because of their subjective evaluation and rejection of the contemporary secular values accepted by the majority, much as Thoreau rejected the social values of his time and isolated himself at Walden Pond, their claims would not rest on a religious basis. Thoreau's choice was philosophical and personal rather than religious, and such belief does not rise to the demands of the Religion Clauses.[29]

Jeffersonian rationalism, which is a deep *religious* conviction about the meaning of life, could not be expressed more clearly than in this confession from the Chief Justice. The "secular values of the majority," he believes wholeheartedly, ought to have moral authority over "society as a whole." Only if a person or group can appeal to the religion clauses with a (sufficiently private) religion, recognizable as "religion" by the Justices, can that person or group find relief from the requirement of majoritarian control within the public domain. Thus the appeal here not only presupposes the religious/secular assumption but also the distinction between "private diversity and public unity" and the belief that the state alone should have authoritative control over any education which is not part of a religion approved by the Court.

Justice Burger, of course, has not demonstrated why the Amish way of life is religious while his own Jeffersonian rationalism is not religious. Nor has he explained his grounds for reducing Thoreau's deep convictions to nonreligious ones, when in fact Thoreau's personal and quite integral life was a religious commitment of the highest order. Nor has he explained why he contrasts an Amish *community* with an *individual person* (Thoreau), when these are two different kinds of human realities.

Justice Douglas points out in his dissenting opinion that Burger's contrast between religion and nonreligion no longer has validity in any case after the Court's decisions in United States v. Seeger, 380 U.S. 163 (1965), and in Welsh v. United States, 398 U.S. 333 (1970). In these cases, which did not deal with education but with conscientious objection to the Selective Service Act, the Court argued that a test for religious belief might be stated as follows: "A sincere and meaningful belief which occupies in the life of its possessor a place parallel to that filled by the God of those admittedly qualifying for the exemption."[30] In other words, the Court refused to put itself in the position of having to define what is and what is not a religious belief and decided to leave that up to the believer.

In 1975 the Supreme Court handed down its decision in the case of *Meek et al.* v. *Pittenger.*[31] In it the Court once again examined whether the establishment clause of the First Amendment had some bearing on a Pennsylvania law that provided auxiliary services to nonpublic schools. Again the Court made its judgment by trying to distinguish allowable secular services from those services which might be ideological or religious in character. The majority decision, in essence, was to allow textbook loans but to disallow other services that Pennsylvania was trying to supply, such as counseling, testing, psychological services, speech and hearing therapy, etc.

In part, the decision reaffirmed the three-part test which Chief Justice Burger had outlined in *Lemon I.* In addition, Justice Brennan referred back to the "fourth test," which Burger first enunciated in *Lemon I,* concerning the "divisive political potential" of state aid to parochial education. But this time Burger strongly objects to the appeal to "divisive political potential" as a

reason for denying certain services to nonpublic schools, especially remedial, therapeutic tools. In this case Burger is convinced
that no potentially divisive entanglement is evident. This only
shows how relative and subjective are "standards" and "tests"
which the Court continues to affirm. The Justices reiterate these
"standards" as though they are sure guides toward judicially sound
decisions. But the Justices take different sides on different cases
that come before them because they cannot agree from one case
to the next on what really constitutes "entanglement" or "neutrality" or "divisiveness" or "aid to religion."

As if to emphasize the Court's confusion, Justice Rehnquist
chastizes the Court in a way that demonstrates how little progress
it has made since the 1940s:

> The Court apparently believes that the Establishment Clause
> of the First Amendment not only mandates religious neu-
> trality on the part of government but also requires that this
> Court go further and throw its weight on the side of those
> who believe that our society as a whole should be a purely
> secular one. Nothing in the first Amendment or in the cases
> interpreting it requires such an extreme approach to this
> difficult question, and "[a]ny interpretation of [the Estab-
> lishment Clause] and constitutional values it serves must
> also take account of the free exercise clause and the values
> it serves." P. Kauper, *Religion and the Constitution* 79
> (1964). . . .
> The failure of the majority to justify the differing ap-
> proaches to textbooks and instructional materials and
> equipment in the above respect is symptomatic of its failure
> even to attempt to distinguish the Pennsylvania textbook
> loan program, which it upholds, from the Pennsylvania in-
> structional materials and equipment loan program, which
> it finds unconstitutional.[32]

The most recent cases the Court has handled in this area
reveal no new patterns of judicial reasoning or attempts to construct better standards and tests. In *Roemer et al.* v. *Board of
Public Works of Maryland et al.*, *Wolman et al.* v. *Walter et al.*,
and *Committee* v. *Reagan*,[33] the Court reaffirmed its commitment
to the three-part test hammered out in the foregoing decades.
The Court continues to indicate its concern for the "potential political divisiveness" of state aid programs. Justice Blackmun, in
fact, in the majority opinion in *Roemer*, states that

> there is little room for further refinement of the principles
> governing public aid to church-affiliated private schools. Our
> purpose is not to unsettle those principles, so recently re-

affirmed, see *Meek v. Pittenger, supra,* or to expand upon them substantially, but merely to insure that they are faithfully applied in this case.[34]

Nonetheless, in *Roemer* Justices Brennan, Marshall, Stewart, and Stevens all dissent from the decision of the majority to uphold state aid to private colleges (including religious colleges) because such aid appears very clearly to them to be aid to religion as well as governmental entanglement. The "tests" were affirmed by all, but the Court stood divided.

In *Wolman* the problem is again that of state aid to private elementary and secondary education (in Ohio), and the decision has the appearance of an odd collection of familiar bits and pieces without any overarching coherency or rationale. Each of the Justices decided to support different parts of the Ohio aid program and to disapprove other parts. Justice Blackmun's main opinion for the Court concluded this way:

> In summary, we hold constitutional those portions of the Ohio statue authorizing the State to provide nonpublic school pupils with books, standardized testing and scoring, diagnostic services, and therapeutic and remedial services. We hold unconstitutional those portions relating to instructional materials and equipment and field trip services.[35]

The Justices who dissent do so in part because they are convinced that some of the approved aid as well as some that is disapproved will entangle the state in religion, or aid religion, or contribute to "a divisive political potential" because of the amount of aid involved.

Justice Powell admits that "Our decisions in this troubling area draw lines that often must seem arbitrary." We could no doubt "achieve greater analytical tidiness" if we simply granted that any aid to a "sectarian" school is aid to the "sectarian enterprise as a whole." But, when we recognize that parochial schools have made many public contributions up to the present, and if we realize that our society is not in any real danger of coming under control of sectarian groups or of being divided along religious lines, then it will be "entirely tolerable" to us to suffer a slight "loss of some analytical tidiness" by allowing some public aid to the "secular aspects of private education.[36]

In order to sense the depth of the Court's predicament it is valuable at this point to quote from the dissenting opinion in *Wolman* of Justice John Paul Stevens. Stevens is completely unconvinced that the Court has made progress from the *Everson* decision (1947) down to the present, and his brief argument demonstrates that the most crucial terms ("secular," "religious," etc.) have neither lost their ambiguity nor gained precise legal meaning in the course of thirty years. Justice Steven's dissent is more than a dissent; it is both a confession of and an indictment of the Court's failure to demonstrate sound judicial reasoning. Stevens writes that the Establishment Clause of the First Amendment must have a fundamental character in guiding the Court:

> It should not differentiate between direct and indirect subsidies, or between instructional materials like globes and maps on the one hand and instructional materials like textbooks on the other. . . .
>
> This Court's efforts to improve on the *Everson* test have not proved successful. "Corrosive precedents" have left us without firm principles on which to decide these cases. As this case demonstrates, the States have been encouraged to search for new ways of achieving forbidden ends. . . . What should be a "high and impregnable" wall between church and state, has been reduced to a "blurred, indistinct, and variable barrier. . . ." The result has been, as Clarence Darrow predicted, harm to "both the public and the religion that [this aid] would pretend to serve."[37]

CHAPTER 6

RESOLVING THE CONSTITUTIONAL DIFFICULTIES

OVERCOMING THE CONFUSION ABOUT RELIGION

THE cases which we have just examined as examples of the Court's work indicate that the Justices have not so far tried, and apparently do not intend to try, to analyze critically their assumptions (and those of the American public) about religion, education, and the republic in order to discover the root cause of the ambiguities and confusions inherent in our established system of education. Instead, the Justices appear to be willing to work within the framework of assumptions and tests that have already accumulated while simply admitting that they (and we) are faced with "opaque" religion clauses, "paradoxes," "unsuccessful efforts" at applying their tests, and a "lack of analytical tidiness."

If we are to clarify the nature of the constitutional problems before us and to suggest lines of legal reasoning and of political policy making that will help to resolve these problems, we must define more precisely the issues and terms at hand, beginning with the word *religion*.

Through the nineteenth century, *religion* usually referred to what Jefferson would have called private, sectarian religion — the activities and beliefs of different ecclesiastical groups or "sects" that were usually organized for purposes that they themselves designated "religious." At the same time, however, the term *religion* was used to refer to the universal moral foundations and identity of the republic; Americans were a "religious" people whose nation was called and blessed by God. The term *religion* or *religious* in this second sense corresponded to the way in which Jefferson thought of the common, universal morality of the republic.

By the twentieth century, the basic distinction between private, sectarian, religious communities on the one hand and the common, universal, moral republic on the other was well established. But now the common republic was identified as "secular" in contrast to the sectarian "religious" groups. This was especially true in regard to public education and public morality. Thus, when today the Supreme Court uses the terms *secular* or *nonsectarian* or *public* or *neutral* or *nonideological*, it intends to signify the common domain of the republic which embraces citizens merely as citizens, apart from any particular, separating beliefs with which they may be associated in their different private "religions." The difficulty with this terminology is that it presupposes a common universality of the republic which does not exist. It must never be forgotten that the republic in its "universality" has been built upon and guided by doctrines, ideologies, values, and moral convictions that cannot be considered neutral, universal, or common. This cannot be stressed too emphatically. Jefferson's Enlightenment convictions were not universally believed; Protestant America in the nineteenth century (including the "public" schools) did not represent a universal public consensus; and the modern, "common," secular republic does not bind every American citizen together in a truly universal nonreligiousness.[1]

What we do have today in America is a general (not universal) consensus among a large majority that "religion" *should* be a private affair and that a single system of universal, tax-supported education *should* be offered and monopolized by the majoritarian political institutions of the republic. But this ideology, this majority consensus of basic convictions about what a healthy republic should be, does not entirely obscure the fact that its moral content, and the content of the public school curricula, are neither neutral nor universally accepted. The republican ideology and the moral consensus represented in public schools are, at best, the expression of a moral consensus of a *majority*, whether local, regional, or national; whether Jeffersonian, Protestant, or Roman Catholic. The fact of the *non*universality of the public consensus is manifest every time a single individual, having gained access to the Supreme Court, is granted freedom from a requirement that he or she should salute the flag or hear the Bible read in school or give an oath as a condition for holding public office.[2] The absence of a purely secular, universally common, public consensus about life in the republic is underscored by the very existence of nonpublic schools, whether those schools are Catholic parochial schools, private Protestant schools, or secular private schools.

The root cause of the ambiguity in the Court's use of the terms *religious* and *secular* is the same as that in Jefferson's use of the word *religious* to mean two different things. On the one hand, the two terms are used to refer to two distinguishable kinds of institutions: churches and states. On the other hand, *religious* and *secular* are sometimes used, not to designate distinguishable institutional entities, but to describe a commonly shared characteristic of all the institutions in a society.

The republic and the states in the republic, for example, are clearly "religious" in the sense that they are founded upon and guided by principles, convictions, values, and a moral consensus which are not held by everyone, and which cannot be accepted apart from certain presuppositions and beliefs. At the same time, churches and their affiliated institutions are clearly *secular* in the sense that they exist in, and pertain to, this world, whatever their ultimate focus or concern might be. To assume, therefore, that churches or self-designated religious groups are *exclusively religious* or that they have a monopoly on "religion" is to overlook the faith-character, the value-laden character, the moral reality of all people and of all institutions on earth, all of which need freedom from illegitimate public coercion in order to exist.[3] Likewise, to assume that the state is *exclusively secular* or that it has a monopoly on the "secular" in a way that can exclude everything that is not common and universal in this world is to overlook the fact that other institutions and communities have a legitimate and in some cases a prior claim to life in this world.[4] Moreover, a claim of secular universality is a religious (as well as political) claim, and a claim of religious monopoly has public political (as well as religious) implications.

This confusion, arising as it does out of the ambiguity of the terms *religious* and *secular,* is cleared up first by recognizing the identity of distinguishable concrete institutions, namely, political communities (local, state, and national), churches, schools, and families. Having recognized the freedom of each of these, we must also admit that each has its religious and its nonreligious elements.[5] The relationship of the religious and nonreligious elements of these institutions has legal implications for such concepts as "belief," "action," and the "free exercise of religion."

BELIEF AND ACTION

In 1878 the Supreme Court handed down its first judgment with regard to the practice of polygamy among Mormons. The decision in *Reynolds* v. *United States* (98 U.S. 145) was a relatively simple one, arguing that whereas the First Amendment protects the religious *beliefs* of Mormons, including their belief in the legitimacy of polygamy, it does not protect their *actions*, their actual practice of polygamy. Polygamy as a practice was judged to be unconstitutional.[6]

The importance of this decision, for our purposes, is that it reveals the nineteenth-century Court's understanding of religion as a matter of "private belief." As soon as a person acted on his or her belief in a way that did not conform to the habits and will of the public, he or she became subject to the public interest in such a way that legal prohibition was possible. Actions, in other words, even if an inner belief required them, were thought to be subject to the public governing authorities. As late as 1940, in *Cantwell* v. *Connecticut* (310 U.S. 296), the Court still argued that even though freedom of opinion or belief is guaranteed by the First Amendment, "conduct remains subject to regulation for the protection of society."[7]

Between 1878 and 1940, however, the Court was gradually forced to adjust its narrow conception of religion as mere private belief. In 1892 the case of *Church of the Holy Trinity* v. *United States* (143 U.S. 226) brought the Court face to face with a conflict between the free exercise of religion and a congressional statute prohibiting the importation of foreigners as laborers. The Church of the Holy Trinity wanted to hire an English rector, bringing him to this country from England in violation of the law. The court decided in favor of the church, arguing that while church and state may be separated, "religion cannot be separated from the people."[8] The Court realized that religion is more than private belief and may of necessity be related to hiring and employment practices.

In 1925 the Court ruled in favor of several private schools in Oregon and against the state of Oregon in *Pierce* v. *Society of Sisters* (268 U.S. 510). Oregon had passed a law requiring all students to attend public schools. The U.S. Supreme Court ruled that although a state may require education, it may not force children into *public* schools. The free exercise clause prohibits such a violation of the rights of parents, said the Justices in this case. Again it is evident that if religion may legitimately come to expression in the choice of a school by parents, then religion is much more than a mere private belief. Religion is belief that has an unavoidable impact in the public arena.

By 1963 the Court had turned away from the simplistic distinction between "private belief" and "action"; it made this explicit in *Sherbert* v. *Verner* (374 U.S. 398). Mrs. Sherbert was a Seventh-Day Adventist who, before 1959, worked a five-day week in a textile mill. In 1959, however, the mill changed its schedule to a six-day work week, thus interfering with Mrs. Sherbert's practice of rest and worship on Saturdays. She refused to work on Saturdays and was fired. When she applied for unemployment compensation, she was denied benefits because she supposedly had no "good cause" for not working. The Supreme Court ruled, to the contrary, that Mrs. Sherbert was entitled to unemployment compensation since her right to the free exercise of her religion could not be infringed. The ruling that stood against Mrs. Sherbert, said the Court,

> *forces her to choose between following the precepts of her religion and forfeiting benefits, on the one hand, and abandoning one of the precepts of her religion in order to accept work, on the other hand.* Government imposition of such a choice puts the same kind of burden upon the free exercise of religion as would a fine imposed against appellant for her Saturday worship.[9]

The implications of the Court's changing understanding of religion was also evident in its decisions on two school cases, *Engel* and *Schempp*. According to Elwyn A. Smith,

> these opinions recognized that the private-public distinction does not greatly help to define separation between church and state. If "private" means personal opinion and action which affects the public only minimally,. . . religion cannot be considered simply "private." It "is an aspect of human thought and action," wrote Justice Frankfurter, "which profoundly relates the life of man to the world in which he lives" — all of it, politics, economics, social reform.[10]

In its recent *Yoder* decision, the Court once again demonstrated how the "belief-action" dichotomy in connection with family life, education, and religion is a relative matter. Chief Justice Burger argued that the failure of Wisconsin Amish parents to send their children to public high school could not be dealt with simply as an illegal public "action" subject to political and legal restriction. That action was an integral expression of Amish religion — of Amish beliefs. In this case, said Burger, "belief and action cannot be neatly confined in logic-tight compartments."[11]

What we notice in the Court's treatment of the categories of "belief" and "action" from the late nineteenth century to the present is that religion is no longer viewed as a narrowly confined matter of internal opinion.[12] Whereas it is possible to distinguish between church and state, it is not possible to confine religion itself to the inner heart or to church activities alone. Religion, as Justice Frankfurter so ably pointed out, "relates the life of man to the world in which he lives." Thus the free exercise of religion cannot be walled off from education, employment, family life, or politics.

The questions which arise then are these: How can the free exercise of religion be properly protected in a political order where government must establish laws that guard the public welfare as a whole? How free can religious practice become without endangering public justice? How far can the state go in directing and protecting the public without inhibiting or infringing the free exercise of religion?[13] In order to understand the meaning of religion and its free exercise, we must understand that religion exists within the life of families, churches, schools, states, and other groups, institutions, and communities, each of which has its own identity and its own religious element. Religion, in other words, is not something that has standing before the law in itself; religion is what people do as they express and shape their lives through families, churches, schools, political communities, businesses, and so forth.

THE FREE EXERCISE OF RELIGION

We have now established four important facts that converge on the question of the free exercise of religion.

1. The Court faces persistent ambiguity as a result of its effort to place government in a position of "wholesome neutrality" with respect to religion. Especially in connection with the establishment clause of the First Amendment the Court has insisted that government must not aid or entangle itself in religion. But the Court's own "tests" and "standards" do not overcome the problematic ambiguities inherent in the terms *religious, secular, neutral,* and so forth.

2. The Supreme Court has recognized that *religion* may not be defined by the state in a way that leads to unfair advantage or disadvantage for any person who is religious. The free exercise of religion, in other words, requires that the government should be neutral with respect to the very nature of religion or nonreligion.[14]

3. The Court has further acknowledged that religion is much broader and deeper than mere personal opinion or internal belief. The free *exercise* of religion, in other words, implies the freedom to *act*, not simply the freedom to think or to hold a "belief."[15]

4. Religion itself is not a legal or political subject, but is rather an expression or manner of life that belongs to people and institutions. From a legal or constitutional point of view it is not religion that may have standing before the law but people and institutions

with religious (and other) claims who may gain such standing. And this realization takes us back to the ambiguity noted in the first point above. The distinction between the actual institutions of church and state is not the same as the distinction between the "religious" and the "secular." Confusion on this point is one source of the ambiguity that plagues the Supreme Court's reasoning.

Each of these four facts relates in its own way to the others and to the free exercise clause of the First Amendment. The purpose of the First Amendment to the Constitution is to designate certain dimensions of human freedom that the Congress (and now the states) of the United States may not infringe. The two religion clauses are the ones with which we have been primarily concerned, but the actual structure of the First Amendment ties three elements together in one sentence: freedom of religion and the prohibition of congressional interference in religion is the first part; freedom of speech and of the press is the second part; and freedom to assemble and to petition the government for a redress of grievances is the third part.

In all these clauses it is clear that individual persons (and in some cases institutions or groups) are the subjects who are to enjoy the freedoms designated. Speech is not a subject itself, but is a function of human beings, whether of one person using voice or pen, or of a group of persons by means of a newspaper or a publishing corporation. The act of assembling together for the purpose of speaking and listening, or for education, or for organizing, or for drawing up a petition to the government, is not itself a subject, but is a function of persons whose convictions, beliefs, and desires come to expression in the form of organizations, institutions, and petitions. In the context of the whole amendment it is clear that religion should be understood as an expression of human beings who must be free to be religious without governmental interference or prior control. Religion, in other words, from a constitutional point of view, is something that derives originally from human beings, not from governments. If persons decide to speak or not to speak, to assemble or not to assemble, to act religiously or not to act religiously, they do so because of their free choice, not because of governmental imposition. Persons, groups, and institutions must be free to originate speech, assembly, and religious practices.[16]

Since religion is a protected expression of persons and institutions (our fourth fact enumerated above), and since the state may not create an unfair advantage or disadvantage for any person who is religious (number two above), a further conclusion follows. The state has no more authority to define a priori what is properly religious than it has to define a priori what is speech or assembly. Whether or not people are properly using speech, the state may not assume prior control over their speaking. Whether or not people assemble or petition, the state may not claim prior control over their assembling or petitioning. Of course, as soon as people begin practicing their religions or speaking or publishing or assembling or petitioning, the government will be obliged to look after the public health and welfare in a way that will lead to the equitable balancing of all these human expressions in the public arena. But the point is that the government may not act in any way that destroys or interferes with the freedom of persons, groups, and institutions to originate their own speech, religion, and assembly.

In other words (number three above), the right of persons to act religiously may not be abrogated or infringed by the state's *prior* decision about the social or personal confines wherein religious practice must be limited. The Supreme Court has, in fact, already corrected itself over the past eighty years, arguing now that it is not legitimate for the state to define religion a priori as a merely personal, internal "belief." As religious *actions* come to light, the government will indeed have to consider those actions in relation to the actions of all persons, groups, and institutions in society in order to promote a balanced harmony of public justice. But the job of promoting public justice through the balancing and harmonizing of many interests and human cultural expressions is quite different from that of deciding beforehand what may or may not be a legitimate domain of religious practice. Acting religiously in freedom as guaranteed by the First Amendment is a right belonging to persons, groups, and institutions. And they must be given the right *initially* to decide what their religious actions should entail. Prior governmental restriction on the domain or character of religious practice is an unconstitutional encroachment that assumes government superiority *in religion*.

We now can clarify the ambiguity the Supreme Court faces in trying to maintain a "wholesome neutrality" in the government's relationship to religion.

The Court has been working with assumptions that actually keep it from doing justice to the First Amendment's demands. Recognizing that the Court's assumptions have been essentially those of Jefferson, Madison, and the majority of the American public only helps to explain why those assumptions have been held so firmly and uncritically; it does not justify them. "Wholesome neutrality" may indeed be what the government should hold as its standard regarding religion, but that neutrality must now be conceived in the context of the four points made above. "Religion" must not be defined a priori as a subject in itself, and particularly not as something identical to, or exhausted by, or monopolized by churches, sects, and so-called "religious" organizations. Moreover, the religious practices with regard to which the government must remain neutral are those practices which people themselves must be free to claim as religious. And perhaps even more important, the government may not lay a prior claim to being nonreligious or to having a monopoly on the secular. All that the First Amendment allows and requires is that the government perform its function so as not to interfere unjustly with the religious, communicative, and social freedoms of its citizens. That task does not carry with it any *prior* right for the government to define what is "religious" and what is "secular."[17] On the contrary, the people themselves may lay an original claim to First Amendment practices which the state may not abrogate or infringe in a prior fashion.

Thus, if a group in the United States claims that its religion requires it to educate its children in its own schools, the government may not abridge that freedom by a prior claim that education is not religious or that the government has a prior right to control education. By the same token, if a group claims that its desire not to be religious (or its desire simply to be free in speech and assembly) requires that it educate its children in schools with a special kind of charter, the government may not abridge that right by saying that education is a prior governmental monopoly by virtue of the government's claim to a monopoly over the secular public welfare.

The state may well decide that it has an interest in education because of its desire to have a literate citizenry. But the freedoms of religion, speech, and assembly guaranteed by the First Amendment do not allow the government to stake a *prior* claim to the terrain of education if in fact its citizens are laying claim to educational freedom as an expression of their First Amendment liberties.[18]

Our argument can perhaps best be illustrated by turning again to the Supreme Court's decision in *Yoder*. Chief Justice Burger's opinion reveals clearly the Court's acknowledgement that the free exercise of religion on the part of citizens may legitimately include educational activities (our third point above). "Amish objection to formal education beyond the eighth grade," he says, is firmly grounded in these central religious concepts. They object to the [public] high school, and higher education generally, because the values they teach are in marked variance with Amish values and the Amish way of life.[19]

The Amish, by right of the First Amendment, have a legitimate prior claim to religious (as well as communicative and social) freedom that the state and federal governments may not infringe. Thus Burger supports Amish freedom from certain levels of compulsory public education because "the values and programs of the modern secondary school are in sharp conflict with the fundamental mode of life mandated by the Amish religion."[20] Burger continues:

As the record shows, compulsory school attendance to age 16 for Amish children carries with it a very real threat of undermining the Amish community and religious practice as they exist today; they must either abandon belief and be assimilated into society at large, or be forced to migrate to some other and more tolerant region.[21]

It is also clear in this decision that the Court is not assuming any right to decide whether the Amish religion is really "religious" or whether it is modern or traditional, pious or impious. This relates to our second point above. The Court has merely given standing to persons making a religious claim and has dealt with that claim on its own merits.

Moreover, in connection with our fourth point, it is apparent in *Yoder* that the Court dealt with the Amish as a *community* of *families* in relation to state *school* requirements. Apart from the validity or invalidity of Justice Burger's effort to distinguish the Amish religious claim from other possible claims that would have been merely "secular" (Thoreau), the fact is that the Amish did make a religious claim, and the Court had to face the real requirements and characteristics of their community and family life in relation to Wisconsin school requirements. Whether or not the Court could distinguish a "religious" from a "secular" realm in general is irrelevant. Thus, the main thrust of *Yoder* is not affected by the Court's ambiguity and confusion regarding the meaning and identity of the "religious" and the "secular." The Court's decision is basically a reiteration of the established point that in spite of the state's "high responsibility for education of its children," it must "yield to the right of parents to provide an equivalent education in a privately operated system."[22]

The meaning of the free exercise clause for education implies more, however. We have already shown in our historical account of the rise of state-supported compulsory public school systems that schools existed *prior* to the state takeover and establishment of bureaucratically centralized tax-supported schools. Schools organized by local groups, churches, or parents flourished long before the state-run schools were established. In the United States, as one example, schools that we now call "private" have existed continuously from the earliest colonial period to the present day, and most of those schools during most of that time have served a very broad public purpose.

How can justice be done to both state and nonstate schools in light of the First Amendment. Justice Burger offers an answer to this question in one of his arguments in the *Meek* case. In it he disagrees with the majority opinion that refused to allow aid for auxiliary services to handicapped children in private schools. Burger's objection is this:

> The melancholy consequence of what the Court does today is to force the parent to choose between the "free exercise" of a religious belief by opting for a sectarian education for his child or to forego the opportunity for his child to learn to cope with—or overcome—serious congenital learning handicaps, through remedial assistance financed by his taxes. Affluent parents, by employing private teaching specialists, will be able to cope with this denial of equal protection, which is for me, a gross violation of Fourteenth Amendment rights, but all others will be forced to make a choice between their judgment as to their children's spiritual needs and their temporal need for special remedial learning assistance. One can only hope that, at some future date, the Court will come to a more enlightened and tolerant view of the First Amendment's guarantee of free exercise of religion, thus eliminating the denial of equal protection to children in church-sponsored schools, and take a more realistic view that carefully limited aid to children is not a step toward establishing a state religion—at least while this Court sits.[23]

Burger's argument is set in a very narrow context, but it is essentially an argument from the principle of financial equity in the face of a state-imposed obligation. Parents, in other words, have little choice about sending their children to school under present state laws. Given that compulsory fact, parents who have a handicapped child are at an unfair disadvantage if they want to send that child to a school where the state disallows remedial aid. But this argument can be immediately enlarged to extend the principle of equity to the full range of governmentally imposed obligations. Is it not the case that, apart from any physical or mental handicap, parents who want to send a child to a nonstate school are at a disadvantage because school taxes do not flow to that school? Apart from whether or not parents can afford to pay extra tuition on top of public school taxes, those who want to choose nonstate schools are confronted immediately with the financial inequity that forces them to choose between "free" or "costly" education in circumstances where the state says that they must in any case choose *some* education for their children. In the case of the poor, there is obviously no choice at all, but even for the rich the choice is built on inequity.

Posing the problem this way demonstrates that justice and equity in education go far beyond the religion clauses of the First Amendment, though they may well be related to the religion clauses as in the Amish case. If a local, state, or federal government wants to require schooling, or to set up schools, or to guarantee education for its citizens, there is no constitutional reason why it cannot initiate such a project. But according to the First Amendment, there are constitutional reasons why governments may *not* infringe the right that citizens have to establish schools of their own choice (for religious or other reasons) without any unjust penalty. Even if "private" schools had not existed before the time of the public schools, the First Amendment would still guarantee citizens the rights of free religion, free expression, and free assembly that might lead to the organizing of schools.

Faced with many kinds of schools, both private and state-run, the government has the obligation to establish and execute laws that will not infringe any rights that are guaranteed by the First Amendment. If the government decides to require education of its citizens, such an obligation must be imposed so that every parent and school (state-run or nonstate) feels the weight equitably. Not only is the free exercise of religion infringed by a government requirement that does not allow poor parents the option of sending their children to a religious school, but the freedoms of speech and assembly are infringed when parents may only send their children to a nonstate school by paying tuition for that school in addition to the school taxes that they are required to pay for the "public" school that they do not use.

Stephen Arons makes this point when he argues that the equal protection clause of the Fourteenth Amendment (to which Burger refers) "condemns making the exercise of fundamental rights depend upon classifications based on economic status."[24] *Sherbert* firmly established this principle when the Court held that "conditions upon public benefits cannot be sustained if they so operate, whatever their purpose, as to inhibit or deter the exercise of First Amendment freedoms."[25] Arons elaborates:

> The state provides "free" public education to all children of appropriate age and qualifications through its system of public schools. But the state may not condition the provision of this education — whether it be a right or a privilege — upon the sacrifice by parents of their First Amendment rights. Yet this is precisely the effect of a school system that requires a child to attend a school controlled by a majority of the public in order to receive a "free" education. The public school will represent and attempt to inculcate values that a particular family may find abhorrent to its own basic beliefs and way of life. The family is then faced with the choice of (1) abandoning its beliefs in order to gain the benefit of a state-subsidized education, or (2) forfeiting the proffered government benefit in order to preserve the family belief structure from government interference.[26]

Arons has explained in his brilliant article the importance of the *Pierce* case for the question of equity in education. His First Amendment reading of *Pierce,* which follows several lines of the Court's own use of *Pierce,* leads to conclusions similar to those which follow from our attempt to draw together several lines of argument about the free exercise of religion and the task of government:

> First, a state's school-financing system may not condition the provision of free education upon the sacrifice of First Amendment rights. Second, a state may not, consistently with the Equal Protection Clause of the Fourteenth Amendment, permit educational choice for affluent parents while inhibiting it for poor parents. Third, state regulation of private schools may not substantially affect value inculcation within them unless there is a compelling state justification for doing so.[27]

FAMILY, SCHOOL, CHURCH, AND STATE

Taking into account all the lines of argument presented in this and the previous chapter, we can see both the great value of the First and Fourteenth Amendments for education as well as the limits of those amendments when it comes to clarifying the rightful place and identity of families, schools, and churches in society.

Historically our states and now the United States have recognized the prior right and freedom of parents regarding the education of their children. This is one of the main lines of legal precedent from *Pierce* to the present.[28] And yet parents who have chosen nonstate schools have suffered the financial discrimination of being able to exercise that choice only if they have been able and willing to pay school tuition on top of school taxes. Clearly, parental rights and freedoms have not been guaranteed on an equitable basis. Governments have, unconstitutionally, assumed the prior right to determine the educational framework within which parents may make their limited, inequitable freedom of choice.

We have also seen that the states may not monopolize education to the point of prohibiting nonstate schools. *Pierce* made it clear that schools of all varieties have a right to exist. But schools other than state schools have suffered the injustice of systematic public discrimination, at least at the level of financial inequity.

Local communities, states, and the federal government have all gone to great lengths to give equitable freedom to a great variety of churches and other religious organizations, granting them equal fire and police protection, nontaxable property, and a variety of other encouragements. But when any of these same religious organizations has established a school, it has been systematically discriminated against in favor of state-run schools.

All of this has transpired, we now know, because the Constitution was established and subsequently interpreted under the influence of the Jeffersonian, Madisonian idea of the republic which did not adequately take into account the identity of groups, communities, and institutions (families, churches, schools, businesses). The assumption was that if individuals were guaranteed certain private and public freedoms, they would then be able to live happily in a republic directed by the moral will of the majority. No effort was made to give constitutional recognition to any "subjects" other than "individuals" and the "political entities" through which they were publicly organized.[29] Thus when, under the influence of Jefferson and others, the republican idea of public education began to grow it only took into account the needs of "individuals" in the context of the "universal republic," not the rights and responsibilities of families, churches, and schools as nonpolitical entities in which individuals also find themselves involved as social creatures.

By the time the weighty legal and political battles over education began to be fought later in the nineteenth century, the problems at issue were (1) the rights of private "religious" schools in relation to the public "nonsectarian" schools, and (2) parental freedom to opt out of the public schools to educate their children at their own expense in private. By this time the historical (but not constitutionally required) assumptions about religion as a private affair and public political life as a purely secular domain were well entrenched. The First Amendment simply was not read from any other point of view. Consequently the government's responsibility to balance the many different rights and freedoms of families, schools, and churches was stifled by the *prior* decision of government to circumscribe the questions that could be asked about education. The government weighed only the public's monopolistic right to educate its citizens on the one hand over against the individual's right to opt out of a public imposition of this kind, at his or her own expense, on the other hand. Both the general freedom of the individual as well as the specific freedom of religious practice were actually tolerated by the public majority only to the extent that they did not conflict with the will of the majority. Thus any education other than public education was legitimately subject to discrimination since it was merely a *private* option *outside* the majority will; it could only be "nonpublic." And given the assumptions about "religion" and the "secular," this discrimination could be rationalized as a legitimate effort of the government to maintain its pure secularity over against an improper establishment of religion.

We have shown, however, that the Supreme Court, following the main lines of public thinking for two hundred years, has worked with assumptions in its interpretation of the First Amendment which cannot be legitimately derived from that amendment. The First Amendment will not allow the state to assume a self-appointed monopoly over the secular, or to identify religion only with churches, or to define a priori the confines of religious practice, or to impose a definition of religion on its citizens, or even to assume that it is itself nonreligious. Having made some of these assumptions (and having corrected only a few of them), the Supreme Court has moved to a point in its decisions dealing with education where the identity of the "school" has been violated or blurred, where parents, churches, and schools have all been handled inequitably, and where the state itself has been left with no consistent and equitable rationale to guide its control of and aid to education.

The problem that we face with the First Amendment is that even if we can clarify and overcome mistaken assumptions about "religion" and "the secular," about free exercise and nonestablishment, and about equity, we still do not have a sufficiently positive constitutional recognition of families, communities, schools, and other groups and institutions. Thus, when governments attempt to aid or encourage education, they do not have (and the

Supreme Court does not have) an adequately developed context of historical precedent within the common law tradition that can guide their decisions concerning the balancing of the many interests and rights of different groups, communities, and institutions.

It is clear at this point in our argument that if the state decides to support education financially, it should do so in a fashion that is equitable for all schools whatever the nature of the community, group, or organization that establishes a school. Further questions naturally arise: How can government distinguish a school from something that is not a school or from something only pretending to be a school? How can the government deal equitably with parents, schools, supporting organizations, and the public's larger interests? How in fact should the government aid all schools equitably, particularly in regard to financing? The answers to these questions lie beyond the constitutional issues of the protections and prohibitions of the First Amendment; they call for a fuller view of society and of the public trust.

Several other democratic countries have attempted to work out such a view. We turn now to their experiences in dealing with education in an equitable, pluralistic manner that contributes at the same time to the public health and justice of the nation as a whole.

CHAPTER **7**

STATE AND EDUCATION: EUROPEAN ALTERNATIVES

Even assuming that the analysis of the preceding chapters is correct, it is natural to be skeptical about the possibility of changing the existing political-educational order. Citizens of most countries are inclined to regard the major institutions of their society as stable and permanent; they find it difficult to imagine alternatives to them. The mere existence of a particular social institution renders it largely immune from fundamental tampering.[1]

This inertia may be less pronounced in this country today than it once was, due to the furious pace of social change which has altered the face of America in the past twenty-five years. Maintaining a static society, keeping things as they have always been, has always been less prominent in American culture than in other societies; it is more improbable now than ever. Indeed, even those conservatives most bent on preserving the social landscape occasionally find it necessary to advocate the most far-reaching changes of all.

But even when citizens lose confidence in the enduring permanence of their social institutions, they do not necessarily question the basic value of those institutions nor demonstrate a willingness to alter them radically. Regardless of the manifest deficiencies of the status quo, people resist change until they are convinced of a better way to achieve the same ends. This chapter examines some other existing political-educational systems which not only avoid many of the inherent ambiguities of our tradition, but also contribute to a healthier development of both democratic politics and education. Though such systems may not be entirely appropriate models for America, they can rid us of the paralyzing assumption that no other solutions are possible and provide a

stimulating basis from which to consider our own future course
of action.

THE NATURE OF DEMOCRACY

Many Americans, if asked, would agree that there is only one
kind of democracy. To be sure, each country has its own special
configuration — Great Britain somehow utilizes a monarch, other
countries get along with multi-party systems and ombudsmen —
but in the end the basic structure seems pretty much the same in
any democracy.

Until recently, scholarly perceptions were only somewhat
more refined: they identified only one *successful* kind of democracy. For example, Gabriel Almond's classification, highly influential in this country in the 1950s and 1960s, identified two basic
democratic systems: one worked most of the time and was stable
(the "Anglo-American type") and one frequently did not work
and was unstable (the "continental European system").[2] Almond's harsh evaluation of the continental system focused on its
alleged "ideological style of politics, immobilism in policy making
and . . . erosion of democratic legitimacy and stability."[3]

Later work by the so-called structural-functionalist school
of social scientists and such scholars as Seymour Martin Lipset
reconfirmed the Anglo-American type as the desirable norm for
democracy.[4] This kind of academic tunnel vision led Benjamin
Barber, as a result of his own work on the unique democratic
tradition of the Swiss canton of Graubunden, to comment acidly
on "an Anglo-American tradition that is as insular as it is fertile,
as narrow as it is long, as dogmatic as it is convincing."[5]

Barber's work was preceded by that of the well-known Dutch
scholar, Arend Lijphart. Lijphart categorizes four possible types
of democratic political systems:

1. Centripetal: systems with a homogeneous political culture
   and competing elites (the United States, Great Britain).
2. Centrifugal: systems with fragmented political cultures and
   competing elites (France, the second Austrian republic).
3. Consociational: systems with fragmented political cultures
   and coalescent elites (Netherlands, Switzerland).
4. Depoliticized: systems with homogeneous political cultures
   and coalescent elites (the system of the future in the West).[6]

Another European, Jurg Steiner, posits two basic models of
democracy, based on patterns of political decision making. One
is the familiar Anglo-American majoritarian model (Lijphart's

centripetal type) in which decision making is concluded by a majority vote. The other resembles Lijphart's consociational model in which discussion on policy continues until all parties agree on a solution.[7]

These and other works have made the scholarly world aware — if uncomprehending and unappreciative — of a different form of democracy which not only "works," but which incorporates practices that antedate the foundation of the better known types of democracy.[8] It is now generally referred to as "consociational democracy," and though its place in the literature is now assured, it remains a *terra incognita* to many professional political scientists and most politicians in the Anglo-American world.

Although consociational democracy is subject to various definitions and variations, we will simply understand it to be the system found in Austria, Belgium, the Netherlands, and Switzerland. The most remarkable fact about the societies of these four countries is their cultural diversity. The phrase "cultural diversity" is deceptively familiar to Americans, raised as they are on notions of ethnic, racial, religious, and regional variety. However, there are two major differences between consociational and American pluralism.

First, though it is easy to recognize the cultural diversity of America — in dress, food, ethnic festivals, etc. — such diversity is not a major part of the *public* order; it is preeminently a private matter. An Italian-American neighborhood's penchant for certain ethnic customs, for example, has no bearing on the official civic life of that community. Consociational pluralism, by contrast, though it respects private differences, also recognizes cultural diversity as a fact of public, legal, institutional significance. Depending on the country and the cultural group in question, social diversity may be reflected in such institutions as newspapers, hospitals, radio and television broadcasting, trade unions and other occupational reference groups, social service agencies, agricultural loan banks, political parties, and of course, schools.[9] In short, though the sponsoring group may be one that would be identified as "private" in America (a group of Roman Catholics, for example), what it produces (a Roman Catholic trade union) is as legitimate and *public* as the AFL-CIO and is part of what it means to be authentically Austrian, Belgian, Dutch, or Swiss.

Second, the cultural pluralism of consociational democracy has a cumulative, reinforcing character to it; there is a tendency for individuals to participate in a set of social institutions which reflect a common cultural complexion. An Austrian socialist, for example, has the chance to be a member of a socialist political party, join a socialist trade union, read a socialist newspaper, live in an apartment operated by a socialist cooperative, take exercise with a socialist hiking club, watch his wife go off to a socialist woman's organization, and be buried by a socialist burial society.[10] As one American observer of the citizens in a consociational democracy comments, "There is an urge for them to formulate a point of view and to define it in relation to other convictions. The consequences are seen in everyday life. *The diversity is apparent in the great number of organizations of different shades of conviction.*"[11] The resulting possibility for a consociational citizen is a fully integrated life within a dense network of mutually supportive institutions. These are the *lager* (camps) of Austria, the *zuilen* (pillars) of the Netherlands, the *familles spirituelles* (spiritual families) of Beligum, and the linguistically (and sometimes religiously) homogeneous cantons of the Swiss. Of the Swiss, Rickover observes that "preservation and cultivation of their cultural diversity is the bedrock upon which they have built their national life, the indispensable condition for the continued existence of their multi-racial state."[12]

The contrast with American society could hardly be greater. America is, with minor exceptions, functionally homogeneous. That is, public institutions are universal in character; they are set up and run in such a way that all segments of the population are supposed to feel fully comfortable using them. A political party established by and for one language group would strike most Americans as unworkable; a distinctively socialist television station would be incomprehensible; and multiple, publicly funded school systems would seem profoundly "un-American." Attempts to transcend our public universalism by means of "third" political parties or alternative schools are kept at arm's length, sometimes with legal and physical coercion. For all our celebrated diversity, we resist giving free, formal expression to it on the public, institutional side of our lives; given the permissible range of behavior in such matters, we are *one* remarkably homogeneous people.

THE BASIS OF CONSOCIATIONAL DEMOCRACY

What accounts for the success of societies arranged and conducted on the consociational pattern? A thorough answer would require an examination of European culture in general and the national histories of the countries involved in particular. What we shall do instead is suggest what assumptions, attitudes, and inclinations have been most important in nurturing such a robust pub-factors spring from the same sources or have been present in the lic recognition and expression of group identity. Not all these same degree in all four countries — and certainly our description of them is not applicable in all its details for all four countries — but the vital role which they have played is abundantly clear.

The first factor derives equally from Christian and preliberal political traditions: it is the notion of the indivisible character of human social experience, perhaps illustrated best by the unity of life under the aegis of the church prior to the Reformation. In such a world, at least in principle, a citizen experienced worship, play, family, and civic life in a coherent, continuous context rooted ultimately in his religious commitment.

The Peace of Westphalia (1648), even as it helped to shatter the unity of medieval social existence, laid the groundwork for the same idea in a new setting. Its practical solution to the raging religious conflict created by the Reformation was the *amicabilis compositio*, a Europe resembling a checkerboard of Protestant and Catholic territories where the favored faith still defined the public legal order for everyone. Diversity of social existence was now a possibility, though still not within the same territory.

The advent of liberalism eventually undermined the Westphalian half-way settlement. Gradually the autonomous individual, guided only by the voice of universal reason, came to dictate religious preference; religion, formerly the integrator of cultural life, was consigned to the private side of one's existence. The "good" (i.e., "rational") citizen was obligated to participate in the new, presumably neutral and universal consensus on the shape of the public order. Though Christian Europe on the whole capitulated in assigning religion to the periphery, the conviction that religion remained at the core of social life persisted among some groups. Its survival demonstrated, as David Moberg has commented regarding the Netherlands — and consociational societies in general — "that religious and philosophical ideologies provide the foundation upon which society rests."[13] The crucial difference, of course, between medieval and consociational societies is the diversity of religious (and other) viewpoints available as the basis of one's social existence in the latter.

A second factor which helps to explain consociationalism has been the inherent need of such countries to accommodate the cultural diversity which characterizes them. In the Hapsburg Empire, the forerunner of modern Austria, a variety of nationalities were afforded their cultural integrity. Switzerland, a conglomerate of fiercely independent regions and language groups, practiced a similar accommodation of cultural groups in its semiautonomous cantons. Such circumstances constitute a rich historical legacy of cultural pluralism on which these societies still draw. In Belgium, for example, recent constitutional changes have established distinct linguistic regions and the principle of linguistic autonomy. Martin Heisler notes that these changes issue from a belief by a majority of Belgians *that the ethnic cleavage should be regarded as permanent and right.*[14]

A tradition of political pluralism is a necessary complement to the cultural pluralism just described, providing the bridge between the existence of groups and their ability to maintain and express themselves publicly. It has taken a variety of forms, including aggressive regional particularism featuring self-governing localities in the Netherlands and Switzerland.[15] Political pluralism also acknowledges the rights of natural social groups, such as the family, which are, by definition, autonomous within their sphere of competence. Both Roman Catholics and Protestants have stressed the need to provide social space for such groups,[16] and for good reason. As the preceding chapters make clear, the drive of majoritarian democracy is to homogenize the public side of society by ignoring group rights and recognizing only the rights of individuals. This effectively undermines any form of institutional life that is not sanctioned by the prevailing consensus. The triumph of the public school in America is, of course, a particular case in point. In consociational societies, however, Hans Daalder notes that established pluralist traditions have "militated against the individualist and majoritarian assumptions of popular sovereignty," thus preserving the conditions making for truly variegated cultural and political life.[17]

POLITICAL INSTITUTIONS OF CONSOCIATIONAL DEMOCRACY

The political life of the consociational democracies comes naturally out of the conditions just described. Political culture in such societies incorporates a number of attitudes and values. Instead of a single, agreed upon set of attitudes and values to guide public life, such as that which governs political life in America, the different groups which make up society are free to develop their own versions of what public life ought to be. In the pursuit of this task they are free from the encumbrance of an American-style civil religion, a majoritarian political institution which defines and limits the public rights of individuals, groups, and institutions. What exists instead in consociational democracies is a public legal order which takes seriously the rights of individuals, groups, and institutions representing different world and life views. Kurt Shell's comment on the Austrian Socialist Party—the political representative of the socialist *lager* but not of the entire nation—and its unique self concept illustrates the openness in consociational states to confessionally defined political parties:

> The Socialist Party has always claimed to be not a party like the others but a *Gesinnungsgenossenschaft*, a *spiritual community*. . . . The continued adherence to the organization pattern of the mass party has been justified by reference to this concept of the Party as a spiritual community and the insistence that the *Party's main task vis-a-vis its members consisted in their "systematic education to Socialism."*[18]

In the United States, an assumed common political culture and deep-seated consensus about what is politically permissible sustains the practice of majoritarian, winner-take-all democracy. In elections, the winning party obtains *all* the representation for a given district, even if its winning margin is as thin as one vote. The fact that a minor party can rarely win an election means that its supporters are, for all practical purposes, disenfranchised. Legislatively, a similar phenomenon exists: numerical majorities are free, within the limits of the Constitution, to do as they like without any reference to the interests of minorities. All this is tolerable and usually does not result in disorder because the major political participants (never that far apart since they agree on basics of the social order) do not ordinarily perceive the political stakes to be that high. Differences are mostly of emphasis and degree.

A vastly different situation prevails in consociational societies where the pluralistic political culture and the absence of a broad consensus on policy impart an urgency to political life that renders majoritarian, winner-take-all practices intolerable. The consociational alternatives to majortarian rule are "proportionality" and "nonmajoritarianism."[19]

Proportionality takes a variety of forms, though in each case the object is the same: to give the constituent parts of the body politic permanent standing and autonomous spheres of influence removed from controversy, thus avoiding the "If I win then you lose" implications of majoritarian, winner-take-all systems. The most basic form of proportionality is that expressed in the territorial division of a country. Switzerland achieves this by means of conventional geographic federalism with linguistically designated cantons. Belgium has created language regions whose cultural development is supervised by special cultural councils composed of the parliamentary representatives of each language group.[20] Proportionality can take the form of parceling out appointments to public offices, funds for certain services, and air time on government-owned radio and television services to various cultural groups. The most famous example of proportionality occurred in Austria between 1945 and 1966 when the Catholic and Socialist parties agreed to a "Great Coalition" to rule the country. The core of the agreement was the notion of *Proporz*, the division of the government (from seats in the cabinet to top positions in government ministries and nationalized industries) in a way which reflected the standing of the parties in parliament. Adjustments were made after every election to reflect the new, relative standings of the parties.[21]

Another form of proportionality is the system of proportional political representation. The consociational democracies use a system that rewards political parties in proportion to the number of votes they receive instead of assigning all rewards to candidates who are "first past the post." Elections are thereby more a matter of seeing what groups need to be represented and much less a matter of sorting out "winners" and "losers." To give a practical example, a party with the support of 20 percent of the electorate takes one fifth of the parliamentary seats on a regular basis with all of the public voice, visibility, and power which that implies. In a majoritarian system, such a party would be a sure and perpetual loser.

An electoral system based on the principle of proportionality helps to produce an appropriate form for political parties and for the party system. With some representation possible even for minor parties, multiparty systems are the rule. Such parties, without the burden of constructing a diverse (and often contradictory) coalition that majoritarian (or plurality) systems impose, are free to be the kinds of parties which their segments of society expect. Election day presents the voter with number of clearly defined choices, most of which must be taken seriously because the election makes their parliamentary representation a distinct possibility.

Many American political scientists recoil in horror at such a prospect. How, they ask, can the majority (50 percent of the voters plus one) rule when there is no majority or, more accurately, when the electoral system fails to produce one? The consociational answer is that the majority principle is not "the fundamental principle of conflict management and the ultimate source of legitimacy but is an auxiliary expedient to avoid deadlock."[22] The facile reliance on majority rule depends on the existence of a general philosophical and political consensus which, as pointed out in earlier chapters, is often more of an assumption than a reality. Only this general consensus makes it possible for minorities to bear their losses; their positions, after all, are not that far from those of the majority in most cases. In the absence of a consensus of this sort, how do nonmajoritarian democracies function? "In Switzerland, it is common to speak of a 'true Swiss compromise.' By that is meant a solution has been reached as a kind of amicable agreement with the participation of all interested parties."[23]

This "amicable" or "negotiated" agreement without recourse to majorities is not equivalent to the familiar bargaining and compromise in our system. The negotiated agreement resembles an "exchange deal"—*Junctin* is the term used in Austria—in which each side gives in on some question in order to win concessions on a separate issue. This should not be confused with American political compromise, which typically consists of finding a middle ground on a single issue. William Bluhm has described consociational party behavior under such conditions as a

> "pragmatism of *dissensus*," willingness to conclude agreement in a pragmatic manner, to reach compromise for the solution of pressing common problems, *while remaining conscious of deep differences in principle, different visions of the good society (Leitbildec)*.[24]

The accommodation of every group's highest priority is not always possible, and painful decisions inimical to a group's interests may have to be made. The thrust of consociational democracy, however, is to go to extraordinary lengths to avoid such decisions. Belgium has perhaps gone the furthest in such a direction. Its constitution guarantees parity in the cabinet for the two major linguistic groups, as well as protection of "the rights and liberties of ideological and philosophical minorities." It also mandates a "warning bell procedure" to call attention to sensitive cultural legislation, for which special legislative majorities are necessary.[25]

CONSOCIATIONAL DEMOCRACY AND EDUCATION

John Courtney Murray, in a comment on the landmark *Everson* and *McCollum* cases decided by the U.S. Supreme Court, argues that they were understood best as "a clash of basic philosophies of education and democracy."[26] Earlier chapters, proceeding on that assumption, have focused as much on the character of our political system as on our educational system in order to expose fully the roots of our difficulties.[27] At this point, an examination of the educational arrangements of the consociational democracies—especially as they relate to provisions for cultural minorities at the primary and secondary school level — should underscore the intimate relationship between politics and education.

Our special concern with education in the consociational democracies will be to show how they give expression in the schools to the cultural pluralism of their societies. Though each aims at proportionality, the specific arrangements in each country vary significantly.

In Austria, in addition to offering some public school instruction in Slovene, Croatian, and Hungarian, the state encourages educational pluralism especially in the so-called "confessional private schools," run by Roman Catholics. These schools have received some sort of government subsidy off and on since a concordat with the Vatican in 1914. Currently, they fall under the provisions of a law granting a subsidy to schools run by legally recognized churches and religious organizations (not individual congregations or private religious orders). Since 1971, the subsidies have paid for 100 percent of all *personnel* costs, but no others. The subsidy may be granted either by the assignment of a certified teacher, who may be rejected by the private school without reason, or by a salary grant to the school if no teacher can be assigned. It is possible under special circumstances, not likely to be met often, for nonconfessional private schools to receive a similar personnel subsidy.

The present subsidy was granted only over the bitter opposition of the Socialist Party. Its argument, interpreted by Kurt Shell, sounds eerily familar to an American ear: "Those who do not desire to take advantage of the educational services provided by the state should bear the cost themselves; . . . private schools should not be allowed to weaken the public school system by dividing the student body."[28] Other socialist charges branded private schools as "antiprogressive" and "antidemocratic."

Although it may surprise some Americans, our country's educational ideals have not penetrated Austria. The argument of the Austrian socialists indicates a fundamental agreement between them and the supporters of American public schools on their philosophical starting point. Shell makes this clear, noting that

> the Socialist educational ideal is the education of citizens as rational, democratic, human beings who, in sharing a body of basic knowledge, would be equipped to form their own judgment and beliefs. It is therefore hostile to any measure which would weaken the unitary public system of education.[29]

In view of such hostility, the 1971 increase in the Austrian subsidy from 60 to 100 percent of personnel costs indicates the Austrian commitment to proportionality and amicable agreement.

Though recent figures are difficult to obtain, it appears that the confessional private schools account for only 6 percent of the nonuniversity school population in Austria.[30] This is surprising in view of the well developed Roman Catholic *Lager* and the fairly generous state subsidy. One answer might lie in the very strength of the Roman Catholic influence; 89 percent of the population claims at least a nominal affiliation. Roman Catholics also dominate among state school teachers. In 1968, 70 percent of all primary and secondary school teachers belonged to the Roman Catholic teachers union which was especially strong in the traditionally Roman Catholic rural areas.[31] The fact that the state school system is so largely dominated by Roman Catholics removes much of the impetus for a fully developed Roman Catholic school system. According to Kurt Steiner, Roman Catholic lethargy may play a role as well. He rates 32 percent of Austrian Roman Catholics as "merely baptized" and 23 percent as "seasonal."[32]

It is not easy to describe the Swiss approach to education. Historically the individual cantons were responsible for primary education; this resulted in as many arrangements as there were cantons and half cantons (twenty-five). Even today, with a federal presence edging steadily into the picture, there is no federal minister of education, because of "Switzerland's diversity of cultures and the different characteristics of the various regions."[33]

Within a canton, religion and language are the two most important cultural features with which the Swiss are concerned. One oddity, from an American point of view, is that seventeen cantons have constitutionally "established" churches, Geneva being the only one with a strict church and state separation.[34] In certain of these, Fribourg for example, Roman Catholic and Protestant confessional schools constitute the "public schools" of the canton, and many cantons give the prevailing church the right to direct religious instruction, Bible reading, and prayers in the state schools.[35] If enough pupils of a minority religion are present, some cantons (e.g., St. Gall, Vaud, Valais) subsidize confessional schools for them as well. Finally, certain predominantly Roman Catholic cantons make grants of such magnitude to private schools that they may be considered to be virtually part of the state system. As a general rule, however, no nonconfessional private schools are subsidized in Switzerland.

Pluralism is respected in language as well as in religion.

Switzerland has four official languages: German, French, Italian, and Romansch. For educational purposes, the courts have ruled that each region has *a* language and that all immigrants to a region—Swiss or not—must adjust to it.[36] Given the number of languages and language regions, this does not prove unnecessarily restrictive. Subsidies and teacher training from the federal government help to perpetuate the smaller language groups, especially Romansch, which is spoken by just 0.8 percent of the population.

Cultural pluralism so dominates education in Switzerland that it is difficult to compare the number of schools reflecting that pluralism to those that don't. The major language groups all receive instruction in their own tongue; no separate figures are kept for confessional schools since they usually either are the cantonal schools or are heavily subsidized by the cantons. In short, educational pluralism is so much a part of the public side of education that cultural minorities have no incentive to have schools outside of the state system. After examining Swiss education to discover the secret of what he considered to be its pedagogical effectiveness, Hyman Rickover observed that "extraordinary tolerance is practised by linguistic and religious majorities; proportionate to their size, minorities always get more than their share of consideration."[37]

Much of the modern history of education in Belgium has been a history of the struggle of Roman Catholics (comprising 95 percent of the population) to secure recognition and financial justice for their schools. Though the new constitution of 1830 ostensibly provided for the existence of "free" schools outside of the state system, liberal attacks on such schools intensified later in the nineteenth century.[38] These attacks culminated in laws in 1879 and 1881 which prohibited local governments (communes) from funding existing Roman Catholic schools—this at a time when 60 percent of the schoolchildren were enrolled in such schools. Furthermore, Roman Catholics were prohibited from teaching in state-run schools and religious instruction was prohibited in those schools.

Subsequent political action eased these restrictions somewhat and some government funding was even provided for free schools, but the matter was by no means resolved. Liberal and socialists continued to challenge the Roman Catholic schools, arguing "that it is the function of the state to provide a system of 'neutral' schools that everyone may attend and that it is the supreme duty of the state, in providing such schools, to safeguard both political and religious freedom for all."[39] Finally in 1954 a socialist dominated government withdrew the subsidies and the right to confer graduation certificates. This attempt to squeeze the free schools out of existence reopened the controversy with all its old fervor.

The issue was resolved in 1958 by the passage of a "schools pact" that offered three particularly interesting provisions.

First, parents now have the explicit right to decide on the character of education their children will receive. "This implies that parents will be able to find a school dispensing the kind of education [i.e., education with a particular religious or philosophical perspective] they prefer within a reasonable distance of their homes."[40] A later provision insured that parents who did *not* wish to send their children to nonstate, i.e., Roman Catholic, schools would not be forced to do so. Parents can petition for a Roman Catholic or state school if none exists in their area, and the state is obligated to honor the petitions if certain minimum criteria are met.

Second, in order to make the first right a reality, the state is committed to the support of a dual system of schools: "official" (state) and "free" (nonstate) schools. The latter are in fact Roman Catholic schools; Protestant, Jewish, and other schools have a right to exist, but without government support. Central government subsidies of the free schools include full support of all staff salaries, pensions, and sick benefits at state school levels. Additionally, the state pays a graded, per pupil subsidy to the free schools. What the free schools do not get is money to build new schools or maintain existing ones; some of this is made up through the salaries paid to members of religious orders teaching in the free schools.

The free schools of Beligum are understood best as a special species of public education and not as completely autonomous institutions, like American "private" schools. All matters of educational policy are decided by mutual consultation between local, provincial, church, and national educational authorities. Most policies simply provide for curricula, length of school years, etc., leaving each educational authority free to make its own arrangements.[41]

Third, education in Belgium takes account of local language and culture. The country is divided into two homogeneous language zones (with one major exception), and schools must teach in the prescribed language to qualify for a central government subsidy and to have their diplomas recognized.[42] Special arrangements are made in bilingual greater Brussels, located within the Flemish language region, to teach children in their mother tongue.

In all, approximately 1,200,000 pupils attend Flemish language schools, 800,000 French language schools, and 7,000 German language schools.

An average of 57 percent of all pupils in primary and secondary schools attend free schools. The figure is higher in the Flemish zone. For some types of schools, notably at the entering grades and in technical and commercial secondary education, the free schools enroll nearly 70 percent of all students.[43] These enrollments have remained quite stable over the past twenty-five years.

The "consociational way" in education is fully realized in the Netherlands. The historical path that led the Dutch to the present system has proven a difficult course. Even after the Reformation, the idea of a *corpus christianum* persisted in the Netherlands; membership in the Dutch Reformed Church was closely tied to full citizenship, despite a large Catholic minority.[44] School teachers had to be Dutch Reformed, and children were supposed to be schooled in Calvinist religion to "the glory of God [and] the prosperity of the church and the commonweal."

Under the impact of the Enlightenment, this denominational monopoly was gradually replaced by a secularized, universal Protestantism which was no less urgent and monopolistic in its claims. The full meaning of the transformation was not immediately apparent, however, and

> many a struggle would have to be waged before the Dutch would learn that they had to abandon the idea of spiritual homogeneity in the educational system and to admit that the unity of the nation can be maintained at the same time as spiritual diversity can develop unimpeded.[45]

The culmination of the liberal search for social unity through the vehicle of a highly centralized school system was the Education Act of 1878. The counterattack, which lasted more than thirty-two years, began with the People's Petition directed against the 1878 act, signed by more than 300,000 people. The counterattack was marked by close cooperation between Roman Catholic and Calvinist *zuilen*, both of which considered the liberal educational hegemony anathema.

The present educational pluralism of the Netherlands has its foundation in the major constitutional revisions of 1917. Among other things, the constitution guarantees that schools are free from government direction, that indirect control of free schools (e.g., the closing of a school because water fountains are too high) is not permissible, and that there is to be equity in funding for both state and free schools.

The Primary Education Act of 1920 built on the guarantees of the constitution in four major ways. First, the legal and administrative distinctions between "public" and "private," "state" and "free" education were abolished. *All* schools in the Netherlands are considered to be part of the public (common) effort to provide education. The practical implications of this kind of definition will be made clear below.

Second, in the words of the government itself, parents have the "natural right and duty" to determine the kind of schooling their children should have.[46] Any group of parents may petition their municipality through their own educational association or through an existing institution (e.g., a church) to establish a free primary school that expresses their educational philosophy. The procedure is not meant to be an obstruction: as few as 50 pupils are needed in a community under 50,000 population, 100 in communities of 50–100,000, and 125 in communities over 100,000.[47] The municipality *must* cooperate in founding the school, according to the principle of "automatism." This means either building a school or making a suitable facility available and equipping it. To ensure a serious long-term intent on the part of the parents responsible for the petition, a "performance bond" equal to 15 percent of the building's cost must be posted. If all goes well, the amount is returned with interest in twenty years. Similar conditions now obtain at all other levels, from preschool to university. All indications are that the arrangements work well as a means of providing the free schools requested by various groups. In fact, Theodore Reller complains in his critical assessment of Dutch schools that 300 municipalities have no "neutral" (presumably, state) school, though he concedes that parents wishing such schools have the same clear rights under the law.[48]

Third, absolute equity exists in the funding of all primary schools. All salaries, maintenance, instructional costs, and capital investments for expansion are provided for all schools at levels at least matching those of state schools. The costs of nonstate teacher training schools and schools for exceptional children are also met by the state. In the words of one investigator, "Great care is taken that the general conditions of education—the building, the quality of instruction, the competence and good character of teachers, the salaries—are the same for both public and private schools.[49] Nonstate schools are free to hire personnel over and above state school levels if they bear the cost themselves.

Fourth, the nonstate schools have the freedom to set their basic direction, hire personnel, determine methodology, and act in the administration and retention of pupils. They are bound, though not rigidly, to state standards in routine matters such as teacher/pupil ratios, basic teacher qualifications, basic curriculum design, the length of the school year, and building safety. Central government inspectors have free access to every teacher (state and nonstate) and visit them at least once a year. It should be remembered, however, that the nonstate schools are represented by political parties that take part in the discussions which shape the regulations. Since 1920, a Roman Catholic or Calvinist has usually served as minister of education.

The opportunity for pluralistic education in the Netherlands has been exploited vigorously. In 1850, 77 percent of the primary school population attended state schools.[50] Today, even though each municipality is legally obligated to provide state schools to meet the demand for them, 73 percent of all children attend *nonstate* primary schools. Parallel figures for nursery, general secondary, and technical/vocational schools are 77, 71, and 88 percent. The largest of the nonstate systems is the Roman Catholic, accounting for about 60 percent of the nonstate total. Various Calvinist schools account for 35 percent of the nonstate schools, and independent schools of different persuasions make up the remainder.[51]

The Dutch themselves are quite aware of both the precedent-setting character of their educational arrangements and how well their system serves their society. An official government description of educational life in the country breaks through the usual cautious and antiseptic bureaucratic description to declare:

> The Dutch system of putting public and private schools on an equal footing in both a formal and a material sense is unique, and is to be found in no other country of the world to the same extent. The Dutch public regards it as a prized possession *because it enables every section of the population to give expression in its own way to the spiritual values that it considers of fundamental importance and to make its own contribution to the development of the community.*[52]

The United Nations' Universal Declaration of Human Rights declares that "parents shall have a prior right to choose the kind of education that shall be given their children."[53] The European Convention on Human Rights and Freedoms is even more specific: ". . . in relation to education and teaching, the state shall respect the right of parents to ensure such education and teaching in conformity with their own religious and philosophical convictions."[54] Though the consociational countries, particularly the Netherlands, come close to meeting these ideals, they are by no means exceptional; most major democratic countries make some attempt to translate the edcational rights of families into financial reality.[55]

The United States has been the major exception in this regard for many years.[56] In our pursuit of the Jeffersonian vision of a common, unified public order we have denied full, public legitimacy to nonstate schools and erected formidable financial barriers in the path of parents seeking to educate their children outside of the state school system. Harsh as it may sound, our *de facto* state monopoly in education brings us much closer to the *de jure* state monopoly of the Soviet Union than to the pluralistic, family-oriented educational systems of countries with whom we claim political kinship. At this point at least, the common assumptions of both Jefferson's liberal individualism and Marx's socialist collectivism bear the same bitter fruit.

CHAPTER 8

TOWARD JUSTICE FOR
AMERICAN SCHOOLS

MORE than two hundred years after American independence and more than one hundred years after the rise of the public school system, the continuing (even growing) controversy regarding education in the United States is remarkable. Busing, budget cuts, classroom violence, prayer in public schools, declining test scores, teacher strikes — all of these and other issues are fueling heated debate.

In the late 1970s the public funding of schools became a major political issue. It grew out of such developments as the passage of the Proposition 13 referendum in California. The proposition established a ceiling on local property tax rates, thus forcing the state government to search for supplementary means of funding schools and other local and state services. Similar movements gained momentum in other states where taxpayers were revolting against rising taxes, even though educational services were not always threatened. One of the most radical proposals advanced by some groups in Michigan called for an end to all local property tax support for education. The state government would then have been obligated to establish a voucher system to enable students to "cash in" their state educational vouchers at any school, including non-public schools. The issue here was not only tax revolt but also the demand for greater freedom of choice in education. A similar demand is being heard in California, where campaigns for the establishment of a voucher system continue.[1]

Pressures on the U.S. Congress continue to grow for some kind of tuition tax credit to aid those who are paying school tuition. Such legislation is supported both by middle class families with children in college and by parents who are sending their children to nonpublic elementary and secondary schools. Voices from many sides demand greater freedom of choice and greater variety of educational opportunity at the elementary and secondary levels.

It is clear that Congress, state legislatures, the Supreme Court, and local school boards are facing intense pressure from parents, teachers, students, school administrators, and taxpayers regarding a number of educational issues. Without doubt we are living in a period that will see great changes in American education. We have seen that, within the present American establishment, full justice cannot be done to all schools. The question for this concluding chapter, then, is, What can be done to promote greater public justice for schools in the United States?

The first step that must be taken by citizens and the government is to recognize that First Amendment freedoms should no longer be hedged *in favor of* the state's moral/religious unity and *against* parental and pedagogical responsibilities and freedoms. Our argument throughout has been aimed at the ambiguities and contradictions inherent in the Jeffersonian idea of the state that has produced a majoritarian, civil-religious conformity that violates the First Amendment. With Stephen Arons, we would insist that a conception of public justice must be put into practice that can provide for the expression of parental, educational, and religious freedoms:

> First, a state's school-financing system may not condition the provision of free education upon the sacrifice of First Amendment rights. Second, a state may not, consistently with the Equal Protection Clause of the Fourteenth Amendment, permit educational choice for affluent parents while inhibiting it for poor parents. Third, state regulation of private schools may not substantially affect value inculcation within them unless there is a compelling state justification for doing so.[2]

In order to implement such a concept of justice in education, a more pluralistic concept of the state is necessary. State unity cannot be built on an enforced spiritual or moral conformity. Rather, it must grow as a public legal unity that recognizes the spiritual, moral, and intellectual diversity which actually exists among its citizens. Structurally speaking, the process whereby the church was disestablished in early America ought to be followed now in the realm of education. *The school must be freed from state establishment.* This does not mean that it would be necessary to prohibit the state from running any school system whatsoever; the only requirement is that true equity, proportional justice, should be instituted for all schools. In other words, funding provisions and all other public legal measures must be nondiscriminatory. No favor or penalty ought to be directed toward any particular school or school system. Thus, under this reform a state-run school would become one among many that are recognized as public schools by the government.[3] Change in this direction would move education in America closer to the more equitable patterns exhibited in the European consociational democracies.

Actual disestablishment, recognizing educational pluralism in an equitable fashion, is only the first step, however. Once schools are freed from the unjust distinction between "public" privileged schools and "private" unsupported schools, then many new questions arise which have not been considered previously. An important fundamental question, for example, is, "What is a school?" At the elementary and secondary level in the present system this question is seldom raised because, by definition, a school has been whatever the local governments and state boards of education have established as a school. But once the state no longer possesses the privilege of establishing the "definition" of a school by virtue of its authority to establish *the* school system, then the local, state, and federal governments will have to establish criteria by which to distinquish between schools that are truly schools and institutions claiming to be schools which are not properly schools at all.

The second step toward justice for schools in America, therefore, will be to redefine the nature of public responsibility for education, and it will have to begin with the creation of new and better accreditation procedures. It is not our purpose to attempt that task here, but we are optimistic that this will not be as difficult a process as it might at first seem. There are at least three resources to facilitate this task, some of which we have already pointed to in the foregoing chapters. First, there are the educational practices that existed in the United States prior to the 1840s. By reexamining those practices we can learn a great deal about how governments can recognize a plurality of schools and school systems without supporting fraudulent or illegitimate or racist institutions claiming to be schools. Second, there are pluralistic educational establishments in some of the European states from which we can learn valuable lessons. And third, we have in this country at the present time a highly diverse system of higher education. Among colleges and universities (and even among some preparatory high schools) there are sophisticated accrediting institutions and procedures which demonstrate the power and ability that schools have for independent and critical self-evaluation. Thus, by careful consideration of early American history, some European practices, and contemporary higher educational accreditation procedures in this country, it should be possible to develop criteria and procedures for public recognition of schools and school systems that can guide government oversight without necessitating governmental interference in the internal life of the diverse schools and school systems.[4]

Taking this second step will immediately end the decades-old court struggle to define what is "secular" and what is "sectarian" in nonstate schools. No longer will it be necessary or meaningful for governments to ask whether they can fund lunch programs or audio-visual purchases in nonstate schools. Our argument, in other words, goes beyond the traditional argument on behalf of public assistance for the "secular" aspects of "religious" schools. If schools are freed from inclusion in or exclusion from the state monopoly, then each school and school system can be recognized as a single entity, as an integrated whole. The "religious/secular" distinction will be irrelevant because a school will not have to claim some privileged identity (as "secular" or "nonsectarian") in order to obtain public funds. Then the courts and other public institutions will be able to concentrate their energies on the proper public legal issues of determining what true equity demands for education and deciding what proportional justice demands for a variety of schools and school systems.

Perhaps the most forceful advocates of the separation of school and state are those with a libertarian political philosophy. Murray N. Rothbard, for example, criticizes the nineteenth-century establishment of the public school along lines similar to ours:

> And so the educationists of the mid-nineteenth century saw themselves as using an expanded network of free public schools to shape and render uniform all American citizens, to unify the nation, to assimilate the foreigner, to stamp all citizens as Americans, and to impose cohesion and stability on the often unruly and diverse aspirations of the disparate individuals who make up the country.[5]

But Rothbard and others with a similar philosophy argue for an educational freedom that comes close to separating education almost entirely from any public responsibility whatever. In their view the goal of human life is complete individual freedom, and state control means a limit to that freedom. Libertarians accept as absolute the individualistic side of Jefferson's individualism/universalism ideology; the libertarian argument sees public control as a threat and hindrance to true liberty. As Joel H. Spring puts it, "Men should not exist to be trained and shaped to serve the state but should have the state serving them."[6] For education this means that the government should be kept out of the certification process (granting diplomas, certifying teachers, etc.), compulsory schooling should be abolished, and government should concern itself with nothing except possibly the "levels of competence in reading, writing, and arithmetic."[7]

While we have much sympathy for libertarian criticism of state control over education, the libertarian political philosophy is not adequate, in our view, for understanding the positive task government should perform for education. We believe that human beings are political creatures as well as family creatures, educational creatures, and distinct individuals. While we agree that human beings do not exist *merely* to serve the state, we reject the simplistic notion that the state can exist in a healthy and just manner without having educated citizens to serve it. The libertarian imagines that the chief cause of injustice is the state itself; if individuals can be freed from public control, then all will be well.

At this point we do not intend to advance an ideal blueprint for educational justice in the future. We are willing to leave open the questions about compulsory schooling, teacher certification, the measurement of competence levels, and other requirements. Perhaps state and federal governments do not need to have as much responsibility in these matters as they now have, but eliminating government regulation of the internal life of schools is not the end of the matter. Government's proper concern for educational justice for all its citizens goes beyond this. Government must assume some responsibility for protecting just relations between schools and homes, between schools and industries, between schools and churches, between schools and the various individuals and groups who are served by them. The libertarian argument for freedom from the state does not address these positive responsibilities that government has for shaping a community of public justice. By contrast, we are quite willing to advocate that governments may legitimately approve taxation measures, establish health and safety standards, guard nondiscrimination regulations, and add other requirements from time to time that serve public justice in the realm of education.

Our argument throughout has been simply that education must be recognized for what it is in its own right as part of individual, family, and community responsibilities that are different from the state's concern for its own economic, legal, moral, and civic cohesion. The libertarian argument is correct that schooling cannot be a tool that is totally controlled by the state. On the other hand, if justice is to be achieved for educational freedom and diversity, for parental choice and societal pluralism, then governments must assume real responsibility for shaping a just republic that is structured differently than it has been to date. Public justice will demand that governments continue to work for the proper nurturing of good citizens. We are convinced that part of what justice requires is the recognition and encouragement of a healthy pluralism in the public arena. Government can assume its full responsibility for public justice and for the training of good citizens without having to control and favor a single public school system to the unjust disadvantage of other schools.

The third step toward justice for schools requires that the government give greater recognition to parental responsibility for the education of children. Naturally, parental responsibility changes as children grow older; parental concern at the elementary level is different from that at the college level. If a true diversity of schools is allowed to exist on the basis of the first two steps outlined above, that in itself will be a major step in the direction of helping parents to fulfill their responsibility for the education of their children.[8]

But acknowledging parental responsibility goes beyond simply allowing a plurality of schools to exist. When the government no longer serves as the legal "principal" and "agent" in education but begins to allow parents and free schools to perform those duties, then the government must devote greater attention to public justice for parents. For example, what will justice require for the parents who have handicapped children? What will it require for parents who cannot find a school that meets the needs of their children within the local community? What extra consideration will have to be given to financing the education of children who come from families living in poverty? Does the property tax base for financing elementary and secondary schools discriminate against the poor, the middle class, the rich, or all three classes in different degrees? What is equitable for those who have suffered racial discrimination? What about those families who have many children as compared to those who have few or none?

We must emphasize that it is vitally important that government recognize the nature and identity of family life and its relationship to the training of children. Since children are not merely citizens, not simply wards of the state, then their life in families must be recognized and nurtured in a way that harmonizes formal school education with family life.

At this point our argument can profitably be contrasted to the Marxist perspective of Samuel Bowles and Herbert Gintis.[9] As with certain libertarian arguments, we are sympathetic to much of the work of Bowles and Gintis, especially that which demonstrates the influence of economic developments in shaping American education. Our disagreement, however, comes when Bowles and Gintis argue that revolutionary change in education must begin with *economic* revolution. Their perspective discounts almost entirely the noneconomic characteristics and identity of the family. They manifest little if any awareness of the special meaning of parent-child love and the family nurturing relationship. People, from their perspective, are simply individual members of the work force.

Thus, on the one hand their view of human life is every bit as individualistic as Jefferson's:

> The central prerequisite for personal development — be it physical, emotional, aesthetic, cognitive, or spiritual — lies in the capacity to control the conditions of one's life. Thus a society can foster personal development roughly to the extent that it allows and requires personal interaction along the lines of equal, unified, participatory, and democratic cooperation and struggle.[10]

But as the last sentence begins to suggest, the individualism of Bowles and Gintis is tied to a universal democratic idea of self-determination. Whereas Jefferson's universalism envisioned a republic that would set children free from ecclesiastical, parental, and sectarian, religious biases, Bowles and Gintis have in mind a universal economic revolution that will set individuals free from the confines of capitalist economic structures. In both cases, parents are part of the problem rather than part of the solution to the problem.

Educational reform for Bowles and Gintis, therefore, has little to do with recognizing parental responsibilities:

> The major characteristics of the educational system in the United States today flow directly from its role in producing a work force able and willing to staff occupational positions in the capitalist system. We conclude that the creation of an equal and liberating school system requires a revolutionary transformation of economic life.[11]

The solution envisioned by Bowles and Gintis is surprisingly old fashioned and lacking in radicality; it is the dream of a *majoritarian*, socialistic, democratic revolution that will reorganize the whole society universally, beginning with the economy, thereby setting free all the *individuals* in that society. Such a democratic economic revolution has little to do with nurturing the responsibilities of parents and children, *as parents and children*, in a pluralistic fashion:

> A revolution is a fundamental shift in the structure of power in the social system and, with it, a shift in those aspects of

social life on which power is based and by means of which it is reproduced. A socialist revolution is the shift of control over the process of production from the minority of capitalists, managers, and bureaucrats to the producers themselves. . . .

[T]he new American revolution cannot succeed without being a truly democratic movement which ultimately captures the hearts of the majority of the people.[12]

We certainly agree with Bowles and Gintis that major attention must be given to injustices in society caused by economic imbalance and inequitable structures, but we believe that justice for education requires public policy changes that recognize and enhance the quality of family life and parental responsibility, not those that merely recognize the economy. Their critique is not radical enough to call into question the basic democratic, majoritarian myth that has guided the republic since the days of Jefferson.

The fourth step that must be taken to promote justice for American schools is for state and federal governments to encourage the development of new schools by clarifying the rights, privileges, and responsibilities of founding organizations and cooperating institutions. Once the government no longer grants a monopoly of public funds to a single school system, it will become possible to begin new schools and to bolster older nonpublic schools. Many churches are likely to remain in (or enter) the schooling business. Independent associations of parents will continue to establish schools. Business enterprises and other organizations will probably help to establish schools. Local and state governments are almost certainly going to keep the "public" schools alive.

All of this can become a very healthy, liberating process, because new energy will be put into creative educational ventures. A diversity of schools will promote a rethinking of American economic, social, political, religious life. Marxists such as Bowles and Gintis will be free to develop schools along the lines they propose. Libertarians such as Rothbard will be able to encourage a purer libertarian political philosophy in their schools. Roman Catholics will be able to strengthen their schools once they no longer suffer the financial and legal inequities that they have endured for more than a century. A new climate of public discussion and debate, covering every aspect of American life, will become possible.

Such free diversity will be healthy for the republic as a whole. It will promote a new and vital interaction between a diversity of schools and the full diversity of American institutions, communities, and associations. Unlike the Marxists who believe that an economic revolution must occur before education can be truly reformed, and unlike the libertarians who believe that the school must be completely separated from public control before it can become free, we believe that radical reform and creative freedom in education can arise from the public guarantee of true pluralism and proportional equity.

It is clear that governments must act to protect and enhance this new order. Those suburbs and corporations with the "big money" cannot be allowed to inhibit or destroy the opportunities of smaller parent associations or organizations that wish to start schools. Just as parental responsibilities must be recognized and protected by government, so the interests and concerns of churches, business enterprises, scientific associations, professional organizations, and different racial groups must be recognized and protected in the field of education. The new and clearer definition of the government's responsibility for schools which we proposed in step two above will help to clarify the proper public legal relationship between schools and other institutions and associations in society.

This fourth step will require some gradual redesign of public funding procedures, of the legal identity of schools and their supporting organizations, and of incorporation statutes. Decisions will have to be made about the redistribution of present school properties and of the building of new educational plants, but these changes can be made gradually through new state and federal legislation, state constitutional amendments, and court decisions on various contested issues. The changes do not require the sudden, destructive overthrow of the present order.

If the four steps outlined above are taken, then they will make possible, indirectly, a *fifth step*. If schools are set free to be schools instead of forced to be branches of public bureaucracies, civil religion, civic virtue, and federal, state, and local politics, then they will be free to dedicate themselves to excellence in education.

School administrators can be hired by free schools that want educational leadership rather than by local communities that want to obtain political clout with the state or to render a reward to a local personality. Teachers will be more free to offer their services to the schools they choose rather than to the only available establishment. They will be free to teach rather than be forced to picket and strike and boycott for a new labor contract. Teachers will be free to look for school communities in which they can share similar interests with colleagues rather than be forced to work side by side with teachers who may be incompetent, uncooperative, cynical, or committed to a different view of the educational process. Students will be free to participate in schools that reflect some degree of harmony with their family lives. They will have a variety of educational reasons for attending a particular school rather than be forced by arbitrary geographical reasons to attend the only available local public school. Parent-teacher associations will be genuine associations based on common and freely chosen commitments rather than on accidental and compulsory geographical-political factors.

Schools that do not offer a good educational program will be forced out of existence by competition, because parents will not have to continue sending their children to those schools. Excellence will breed further excellence. Educational reforms and improvements will arise through the natural quest for excellence in dozens of different free schools and school systems; educational standards will not be the sole province of a few state bureaucrats, a few teachers colleges, and a few university scholars dictating from the top down to a captive audience.

Once again our intention is not to try to dictate or predict the course of events once schools are given proportional, equitable, pluralistic freedom within the public arena. We are simply suggesting some of the benefits that will come to the educational process once schools are allowed to be schools, once justice is done to education on its own terms. Schools and school personnel will reap rewards just as families, churches, local communities, state and federal governments, scientific organizations, businesses, and other organizations will all reap rich rewards. We can realistically anticipate growth in educational excellence, public justice, parental dedication, youthful satisfaction, economic efficiency, and much more.

We recognize that not everyone agrees that the development of a pluralistic and equitable system of public funding for schools will improve education and create a more democratic society. While there are increasing numbers of individuals and groups that have become critical of the present system of public education, there are others rallying to its defense. In the minds and hearts of many citizens and public leaders a monopolistic, majoritarian public school system is the only conceivable structure for a democratic society.

R. Freeman Butts, for example, has been one of the leading apologists for the public school establishment in the United States. Butts writes to counter what the title of one article calls "Assaults on a Great Idea."[13] The public schools ("symbols of our secular society") are facing what he describes as:

> the constant downbeat of romantic critics about the horrors perpetrated by public schools upon innocent children; the upswing of effort by religious groups to get public funds; the volatile feelings about busing to overcome segregation; the social scientist dictum that public schools do not reduce inequality or really make much difference in social change at all; the heightening of group feelings among racial and ethnic groups in their search for maintaining or reasserting particularist identities; the revulsion against any kind of authoritative establishmentariarism symbolized by compulsory attendance laws or credentialling; the contests over community versus professional control.[14]

"These and many more specifics," according to Butts, "have transformed the siren call of 'alternatives' into a bullhorn of nonnegotiable demands."[15]

In Butts's defense of the public school establishment we see clearly how his Jeffersonian, Enlightenment commitment shapes his political and educational perspective.[16] He recognizes that the development of the present monopolistic, majoritarian structure of public education has been intricately linked with the triumph of Enlightenment ideology in the emergence of this nation.[17] For Butts this has been a normative development; in other words, it *should* have happened this way. The public schools in the United States have helped to create and maintain a democratic political community in a society made up of diverse ethnic, religious, and cultural groups. Although he is fully aware of people's suspicions and their revulsion against using schools for patriotism, propaganda, partisanship, or politicization, he nevertheless asserts that everyone ought to recognize and accept "the historical underpinnings of the political purpose of public education."[18] To *recognize* and to *accept* the inevitable political purpose of education is the only option Butts offers those individuals and groups that feel helpless and alienated in the midst of the monopolistic and majoritarian educational establishment in the United States.

As the earlier chapters of this study indicate, we believe that Butts is largely correct in his historical assessment of both the roots and the role of public education as it exists today.[19] He is correct that an Enlightenment life-and-world-view *did* guide the political and educational vision of Jefferson and others in the eighteenth century and *did* structure the monopolistic, majoritarian educational establishment that emerged in the nineteenth century. However, we cannot accept Butts's uncritical conclusion that this was a normative development — that this is what *ought* to have happened. The many books and articles that Butts has written stand as a testimony to the origins of precisely those problems that our study has been attempting to resolve.[20] They are a testimony, however, which offers no help toward achieving public justice in an educational arena where many different individuals and groups are left without freedom of choice.

Our point, in brief, is that while there are increasingly more critics of the present educational establishment, there are also many individuals such as Butts who continue to support the existing structure. The present national debate over tuition tax credits and vouchers indicates that the political-educational struggle will continue on many fronts between those who are committed to maintaining the present educational establishment and those who believe that public justice demands the disestablishment of a monopolistic, majoritarian educational structure.

A final question that the reader may have been asking, even as we have asked it many times, is: How can a new order for American education be established; what are the best methods for producing political change, for bringing about financial and legal equity for education? Our reason for not attempting to answer this question is that it is historically inappropriate in our complex federal system to rely on a single set of proposals for change. There is no *single* best method for bringing about change; there are several roads, but no single clear road, to our desired destination. Many different efforts will have to be made all at once, in concert, over a considerable period of time.

The educational framework that now exists is an intricate conglomeration of local, state, and federal political control; there is no single point of attack upon such a complex bulwark. Change will have to be sought through new state and federal legislation; through local, particularly urban, reforms that can become models for other communities; through the courts; through amendment of state constitutions; and through other processes as well.

Disestablishment a second time will require many different kinds of cooperative political efforts made by many groups at all of the levels just mentioned.[21] Legal efforts to get the Supreme Court to interpret the First Amendment properly will be essential, but they cannot stand alone. Efforts to change one or more state constitutions will have to be made, but they will not be sufficient. Federal legislation, such as the 1977–78 and 1981–82 proposals for tuition tax credits,[22] will help to promote equity, but this reform will not come easily. Political strategists will have to bring their most creative energies and insights to bear on the problem of disestablishment for the next decade or more. In the end, such efforts will see public justice done to American schools.

NOTES

INTRODUCTION

1. Bernard Bailyn, *Education in the Forming of American Society* (Chapel Hill: The University of North Carolina Press, 1960), p. 14.
2. Ibid.
3. Michael B. Katz, *Class, Bureaucracy, and Schools: The Illusion of Educational Change in America,* expanded edition (New York: Praeger Publishers, 1971).
4. See for example, William F. Rickenbacker, ed., *The Twelve Year Sentence: Radical Views of Compulsory Schooling* (New York: Dell, 1974).
5. Samuel Bowles and Herbert Gintis, *Schooling in Capitalist America: Educational Reform and the Contradictions of Economic Life* (New York: Harper Colophon Books, 1976).

CHAPTER 1

1. Donald R. Cutler, ed., *The Religious Situation: 1968* (Boston: Beacon Press, 1968) and Russell E. Richey and Donald G. Jones, eds., *American Civil Religion* (New York: Harper and Row, 1974) are collections of essays that demonstrate the nature and extent of the debate about civil religion.
2. Joseph R. Strayer, *Western Europe in the Middle Ages* (New York: Appleton-Century-Crofts, 1950), p. 8.
3. Ibid. See the excellent book by Walter Ullmann, *Medieval Political Thought* (Baltimore: Penguin, 1965).
4. Sir Ernest Barker, *Church, State and Education* (Ann Arbor: University of Michigan Press, 1957), Preface, p. i.
5. Ibid, p. 58.
6. Plato, *Laws,* VII, quoted in Fustelde Coulanges, *The Ancient City: A Study on the Religion, Laws and Institutions of Greece and Rome* (Garden City, New York: Doubleday, 1956), p. 221.
7. William Harrison Woodward, *Vittorino da Feltre and Other Humanist Educators* (Cambridge: The University Press, 1905), p. 100.
8. Nonecclesiastical control and support of education were on the increase in part because Italian towns throughout the Middle Ages had kept control of their ancient municipal academies. The Italian towns also

provided the freedom for lay teachers, like Vittorino, to conduct their own schools. It is reported that in the second half of the thirteenth century as many as eighty secular teachers were working in Milan, and in Florence the numbers were so large the teachers formed one of the largest guilds. See Frederick Eby and Charles Flinn Arrowood, *The History and Philosophy of Education Ancient and Modern* (New York: Prentice-Hall, 1946), p. 819.

9. Frederick Eby, *Early Protestant Educators: The Educational Writings of Martin Luther, John Calvin, and Other Leaders of Protestant Thought* (New York: McGraw-Hill, 1931), p. 5.

10. Ibid., p. 6.

11. For the full text of this letter as well as other of Luther's works on education see F. V .N. Painter, *Luther on Education* (St. Louis: Concordia, 1928).

12. Eby, *Early Protestant Educators*, p. 7. For a fuller discussion of the role of the schools in Calvin's Geneva, consult W. Fred Graham, *The Constructive Revolutionary: John Calvin and his Socio-Economic Impact* (Richmond, Virginia: John Knox Press, 1971), pp. 145–151.

13. Sidney Mead, *The Lively Experiment: The Shaping of Christianity in America* (New York: Harper and Row, 1963), pp. 17, 20.

14. In reference to Plymouth Colony Mead points out that as the colony "prospered it made support of the church compulsory, demanded that voters be certified as 'orthodox in the fundamentals of religion' and passed laws against Quakers and other heretics" (ibid., p. 17).

15. Lawrence A. Cremin makes clear that "the idea that schooling ought to be generally available for the advancement of piety, civility, and learning was accepted throughout the colonies: in New England, that acceptance was manifested by the actual existence of a substantial number of schools; in Virginia and Maryland, where scattered settlements rendered this less feasible, that acceptance was manifested by a continuing concern that more schools be brought into being. . . . Whenever it took root, schooling was viewed as a device for promoting uniformity, and controlling elements of society" (*American Education: The Colonial Experience, 1607–1783* [New York: Harper and Row, 1970], p. 192). Cremin's work is an excellent discussion of the complex history of education in colonial America.

16. For a discussion of the assumptions, traditions, and institutions of late sixteenth- and seventeenth-century English education, see Bailyn, *Education*, pp. 15–29.

17. Act of 1642. The Massachusetts Educational Laws of 1642, 1647, and 1648 are reprinted in David B. Tyack, ed., *Turning Points in American Educational History* (Lexington, Mass.: Xerox College Publishing, 1967), pp. 14–17.

18. The Education Law of 1647 stipulated that every township of fifty householders should provide a teacher "whose wages shall be paid either by the parents or masters of such children, or by the inhabitants in general" and "that where any towne shall increase to the number of 100 families or householders, they shall set up a grammar schoole, the master thereof being able to instruct youth so farr as they may be fitted for the university" (ibid., p. 16). The following year the Massachusetts General Court passed another act setting forth specific penalities for neglect of the two previous laws.

19. Although the Puritans had organized their schools to preserve

and propagate their way of life, it soon became obvious that those efforts were being frustrated by the secularizing forces of the seventeenth century. Will Herberg has pointed out that "nothing is more striking than the fact that, whereas the purpose of Puritan education was Christian, its philosophy and psychology were humanistic, harking back to Athens rather than to Jerusalem." Herberg, "Religion and Education in America," in James Ward Smith and A. Leland Jamison, eds., *Religious Perspectives in American Culture*, Vol. II of *Religion in American Life* (Princeton: Princeton University Press, 1961), p. 15. For a discussion of the role of the Great Awakening and subsequent revival movements in the secularization of education see pp. 12–18. On the meaning and significance of *"paideia"* and of the Greek roots of educational ideas and ideals, see Werner Jaeger, *Paideia: The Ideal of Greek Culture*, 3 vols. (New York: Oxford University Press, 1943–1945).

20. Law of 1642, in Tyack, *Turning Points*, p. 14.

21. Cremin, *American Education*, pp. 181–192, 520–526.

22. Bailyn, *Education*, p. 81. While support for education continued in Boston and other coastal communities, the neglect elsewhere "was so great that in 1718 the General Court condemned those 'many towns that not only are obliged by law, but are very able to support a grammar school, yet choose rather to incurr and pay the fine or penalty than maintain a grammar school,' and raised the fine for negligence to the considerable sum of £30" (ibid., p. 82).

23. For a discussion of the problems of financing public education see ibid., pp. 41–45, 108–112. For example: "Everywhere—in the middle colonies and in the South as well as in New England—the support for schools and even colleges came not from the automatic yield from secure investments but from repeated acts of current donation, whether in the form of taxes, or of individual, family, or community gifts. The autonomy that comes from an independent, reliable, self-perpetuating income was everywhere lacking. The economic basis of self-direction in education failed to develop" (ibid., p. 44).

24. The assumption, as set forth by such nineteenth-century educational historians as Ellwood Cubberly, that the roots of modern public education are to be found in Puritan New England has been forever laid to rest by such contemporary historians as Tyack and Bailyn. Tyack points out that ". . . the Puritan's achievement in education is inseparable from their religious world view and from the trials they encountered in establishing a city upon a hill; it is misleading to read present views of public education into the Puritan experiment. The founding of public education as it is known today would stem from a new world view and new trials in the nineteenth century" (Tyack, *Turning Points*, p. 5). For Bailyn's similar comments see *Education*, pp. 3–16. See also Lawrence Cremin, *The Wonderful World of Ellwood Patterson Cubberly: An Essay on the Historiography of American Education* (New York: Teachers College Press, 1965).

25. Penn's statement is found in "The Preface to Penn's Frame of Government" written in England early in 1682. Extracts are printed in J. P. Wickersham, *A History of Education in Pennsylvania* (New York: Arno Press, 1969 [1886]), pp. 32–33. See also Thomas Woody, *Early Quaker Education in Pennsylvania* (New York: Arno Press, 1969 [1920]).

26. Wickersham, *History of Education in Pennsylvania*, p. 52.

27. Ibid., pp. 53–54.

28. Cremin, *American Education*, p. 306.

29. A statistical summary of the kinds of schools and number of schoolmasters in Philadelphia between 1689 and 1783 can be found in ibid., pp. 538–539.

30. Perry Miller, *Errand Into the Wilderness* (New York: Harper and Row, 1955), p. 126.

31. Sadie Bell, *The Church, the State, and Education in Virginia* (New York: Arno Press, 1969 [1930]), pp. 21–23.

32. Quoted in Cremin, *American Education*, pp. 12–13.

33. Quoted in Bailyn, *Education*, p. 26.

CHAPTER 2

1. Robert Healey, *Jefferson on Religion and Public Education* (New Haven: Yale University Press, 1962), p. 17. See also Daniel Boorstin, *The Lost World of Thomas Jefferson* (Boston: Beacon Press, 1966 [1948]), pp. 27–56.

2. Peter Gay, *The Enlightenment: An Interpretation* (New York: Vintage Books, 1966), p. 55.

3. Jefferson's letter to Peter Carr, Aug. 10, 1787, Appendix V in James B. Conant, *Thomas Jefferson and the Development of American Public Education* (Los Angeles: University of California Press, 1970), p. 102. The letter can also be found in some standard collections of Jefferson's writings, e.g., Julian P. Boyd, ed., *The Papers of Thomas Jefferson*, XII (Princeton: Princeton University Press, 1955), 16; and Saul K. Padover, ed., *The Complete Jefferson* (New York: Duell, Sloan, and Pearce, 1943), pp. 1059–1060.

4. Letter to Adams, Jan. 11, 1817, in H. A. Washington, ed., *The Writings of Thomas Jefferson* (Washington, D.C.: Taylor and Maury, 1854), VII, 56.

5. Healey, *Jefferson*, p. 41.

6. Note the thorough description and analysis of this anthropology in Eric Voegelin, *From Enlightenment to Revolution*, ed. John H. Hallowell (Durham, N.C.: Duke University Press, 1975), pp. 35–73. Some earlier interpretations of Jefferson, especially those of Daniel Boorstin *(The Lost World of Thomas Jefferson)* and Carl Becker *(The Declaration of Independence* [New York: Alfred Knopf, 1966]), emphasized Jefferson's roots in the philosophy of John Locke. Garry Wills (*Inventing America: Jefferson's Declaration of Independence* [New York: Vintage Books, 1978]) has challenged those interpretations by pointing to the distinctive character of Scottish Common Sense moral philosophy which is more likely to have been the primary influence on Jefferson. Our interpretation demonstrates the validity of much of Wills's reinterpretation while refusing to admit too great a difference between Locke and the Scottish realists when it comes to social and political philosophy. For further background see John C. Vanderstelt, *Philosophy and Scripture* (Marlton, N. J.: Mack Publishing Co., 1978), pp. 9–74, and Ernst Cassirer, *The Philosophy of the Enlightenment* (Boston: Beacon Press, 1951), chap. 3, "Psychology and Epistemology."

7. Healey, *Jefferson*, pp. 40–41.

8. Jefferson, *Notes on the State of Virginia* (New York: Harper and Row, 1964), p. 152.

NOTES

9. Letter of Aug. 10, 1787, in Conant, *Thomas Jefferson*, p. 101.

10. Becker, *Declaration of Independence*, p. 39.

11. See Healey, *Jefferson*, p. 174.

12. John Dewey, *Freedom and Culture* (New York: Putnam, 1939), pp. 155–156.

13. Elwyn A. Smith, *Religious Liberty in the United States* (Philadelphia: Fortress Press, 1972), p. 37.

14. Letter of June 13, 1814, in Adrienne Koch and William Peden, eds., *The Life and Selected Writings of Thomas Jefferson* (New York: Modern Library, 1944), p. 636. See Wills, *Inventing America*, pp. 198–206.

15. Becker, *Declaration of Independence*, pp. 74ff.

16. Ibid., p. 57. One of the best studies of the background and development of natural law in connection with its modern influence is Leo Strauss, *Natural Right and History* (Chicago: University of Chicago Press, 1953), esp. pp. 81–251. On Locke see also Basil Willey, *The Seventeenth Century Background* (Garden City, N.Y.: Doubleday Anchor Books, 1953), pp. 263–292, and C. B. Macpherson, *The Political Theory of Possessive Individualism: Hobbes to Locke* (New York: Oxford University Press, 1962), pp. 194–262.

17. Wills, *Inventing America*, p. 175.

18. Becker, *Declaration of Independence*, p. 40. See also Becker's *The Heavenly City of the Eighteenth-Century Philosophers* (New Haven: Yale University Press, 1932), esp. pp. 33–70. Cf. Edward S. Corwin, *The "Higher Law" Background of American Constitutional Law* (Ithaca: Cornell University Press, 1929), p. 59: "Between a universe 'lapt in law' and the human mind all barriers were cast down. Inscrutable deity became scrutable nature. On this basis arose English deism, which, it has been wittily remarked, 'deified Nature and denatured God.' "

19. Letter to James Fishback, Sept. 27, 1809, collected in Saul K. Padover, ed., *Democracy by Thomas Jefferson* (New York: Appleton-Century, 1939), pp. 177–178.

20. Healey, *Jefferson*, p. 160.

21. David Little, "The Origins of Perplexity: Civil Religion and Moral Belief in the Thought of Thomas Jefferson," in Richey and Jones, eds., *American Civil Religion*, p. 200.

22. From a letter to John Adams, Jan. 11, 1817, in Washington, ed., *Writings*, VII, 55.

23. Cf. Little, "Origins of Perplexity," p. 194: "There is no doubt that Jefferson took his own Unitarian position as normative, and, therefore, as superior to all competitors. He fully expected, he said, 'that the present generation will see Unitarianism become the general religion of the United States.' He expected this inevitable upsurge of right religion because, as Americans became liberated from the foolish distractions of theological controversy and, accordingly, more eligible for guidance by sense perceptions, competing religious views would wither away."

24. Healey, *Jefferson*, p. 98. Note Jefferson's letters, cited above, to Thomas Law, June 13, 1814, and to James Fishback, Sept. 27, 1809.

25. For background and further discussion of this argument, see Ernst Cassirer, *The Myth of the State* (New Haven: Yale University Press, 1946), pp. 169–170; Healey, *Jefferson*, p. 115; and Cassirer, *The Philosophy of the Enlightenment*, chap. 4, "Religion," pp. 134–196.

26. For a brief survey of the actual state of affairs, see Cushing

Strout, *The New Heavens and New Earth: Political Religion in America* (New York: Harper and Row, 1974), pp. 50–100.

27. According to Little, Jefferson "was certain that all conventional theological disputes, particularly those making appeals to revelation, were nothing but the 'charlatanry of the mind.' " ("Origins of Perplexity," p. 194). On this subject of revelation and miracles, see especially Jefferson's *The Morals and Life of Jesus of Nazareth*, in Andrew A. Lipscomb and Albert F. Bergh, eds., *Writings of Thomas Jefferson*, XX (Washington, D.C.: The Thomas Jefferson Memorial Association, 1903).

28. Koch and Peden, *Life and Selected Writings*, pp. 705–706.

29. Benjamin Franklin's confession of faith, as another example from this period, fits this same pattern. See Strout, *New Heavens*, p. 80.

30. Cf. Little., "Origins of Perplexity," p. 195: ". . . Jefferson did favor tolerating religious views other than his own, but only because he believed these views were quite irrelevant to the conduct of political affairs, and they would eventually wither away, anyway. But more important, he certainly regarded his religion as the obvious (and inevitable) substitute for all traditional versions of Christianity and by implication, for all other religions."

31. See Jefferson's letter to Thomas Cooper, Nov. 2, 1822, where he explains his desire to have different religious sects represented at the University of Virginia, with each maintaining its independence, to allow them all to mix with the mass of students and thus to "soften their asperities, liberalize and neutralize their prejudices, and make the general religion a religion of peace, reason, and morality," in Washington, ed., *Writings*, VII, 267.

32. See Mark A. Noll, "Christianity and Humanistic Values in Eighteenth-Century America: A Bicentennial Review," *Christian Scholar's Review*, 6 (1976), 114–126; and Nathan O. Hatch, *The Sacred Cause of Liberty: Republican Thought and the Millennium in Revolutionary New England* (New Haven: Yale University Press, 1977).

CHAPTER 3

1. Sidney Mead, *Lively Experiment*, p. 61.

2. Ibid., pp. 57–58.

3. Boorstin, *The Lost World*, p. 195.

4. Ibid., p. 197. Cf. Wills, *Inventing America*, pp. 293–306.

5. Cf. the interpretations of Wills, *Inventing America*, pp. 284–306, and Becker, *Declaration of Independence*, pp. 203–204.

6. Little, "Origins of Perplexity," p. 197.

7. Letter to Baron Von Humboldt, June 13, 1817, in Koch and Peden, *Life and Selected Writings*, p. 681.

8. Quoted in Healey, *Jefferson*, p. 43, from one of Jefferson's opinions written in 1790, in Paul L. Ford, ed., *Writings of Thomas Jefferson*, 10 vols. (New York: The Knickerbocker Press, 1892–1899), V, 205–206.

9. Letter to Dr. William Bache, Feb. 2, 1800, in Koch and Peden, *Life and Writings*, p. 556.

10. Boorstin, *The Lost World*, pp. 200–201.

11. Letter to Colvin, Sept. 20, 1810, in Koch and Peden, *Life and Writings*, pp. 606–607.

12. Mead, *Lively Experiment,* p. 64.

13. Boorstin, *The Lost World,* p. 203.

14. Jefferson's conviction was that "religion is a matter which lies solely between man and his God, that he owes account to none other for his faith or his worship" (ibid, pp. 131–132). James Madison expressed the same idea in his "Memorial and Remonstrance" against a Virginia bill which would have given public financial support for teachers of the Christian religion (1784), when he said that the religion of every man "must be left to the conviction and conscience of every man; and it is the right of every man to exercise it as these may dictate. This right is, in its nature, an unalienable right. It is unalienable because the opinions of men, depending only on the evidence contemplated in their own minds, cannot follow the dictates of other men" (Para. 1).

15. Smith, *Religious Liberty,* p. 46.

16. In his proposed "Act for Establishing Religious Freedom" in Virginia (1786), Jefferson asserted that "our civil rights have no dependence on our religious opinions. . . . All men shall be free to profess, and by argument to maintain, their opinions in matters of religion, and that the same shall in no wise diminish, enlarge, or affect their civil capacities" (Boyd, *Papers,* II, 545–547). Madison's statement in the "Memorial and Remonstrance" is "that in matters of religion no man's right is abridged by the institution of civil society; and *that religion is wholly exempt from its cognizance*" (italics added).

17. For more on Jefferson in this connection, see Smith, *Religious Liberty,* p. 57.

18. Mead, *Lively Experiment,* p. 64. In another book Mead stresses that the "theology of the republic" is distinctly different from the theologies of the particular Protestant religious groups: "To overlook this is to confuse or completely to bypass unresolved theological issues between the denominations and the civil authority. The issue is between the theology of the Republic's legal structure, *which defines even the nature and limits of religious freedom,* and the theology of the denominations, which defines their self-identity and correlative reasons for separate existence" (italics added; Sidney Mead, *The Nation with the Soul of a Church* [New York: Harper Forum Books, 1975], p. 19).

19. According to Mead, Jefferson (and other rationalists) "held that only what is common to all religions and all sects . . . is relevant to the being and well-being of the *commonwealth.* This is the theology behind the legal structure of America, the theology on which the practice of religious freedom is based and its meaning interpreted. Under it, one might say, it is religious particularity, Protestant or otherwise, that is heretical and schismatic — even un-American" (*Nation with the Soul,* p. 22).

20. Mead, *Lively Experiment,* pp. 60–61.

21. Accepting this framework, says Mead, had the following implication: ". . . to become 'American' has always meant, implicitly at least, to accept the theology of America's creed and to renounce traditional particularity along with the devil of sectarianism and all his works" (*Nation with the Soul,* pp. 22–23). Mark DeWolfe Howe argues similarly in his *The Garden and the Wilderness* (Chicago: University of Chicago Press, 1965), pp. 2, 6, 18, 19.

22. Mead, *Nation with the Soul,* p. 69.

23. Leonard Levy points out, with regard to "liberty" for example, that "in all his [Jefferson's] writings, over a period of fifty years of high

productivity, there is not a single sustained analysis of liberty" ("Jefferson as a Civil Libertarian," in Lally Weymouth, ed., *Thomas Jefferson: the Man, His World, His Influence* [New York: Putnam's Sons, 1973], p. 213).

24. Jefferson, *Notes on the State of Virginia*, p. 138.

25. Robert D. Heslep, *Thomas Jefferson and Education* (New York: Random House, 1969), p. 88. See also Roy J. Honeywell, *The Educational Work of Thomas Jefferson* (Cambridge: Harvard University Press, 1931), p. 148.

26. Tyack, ed., *Turning Points*, p. 84.

27. Jefferson's bill can be found in Conant, *Thomas Jefferson*, pp. 89–93.

28. Ibid., pp. 3–11. See also Honeywell, *Educational Work*, pp. 148–149.

29. Healey, *Jefferson*, p. 187.

30. Conant, *Thomas Jefferson*, pp. 17–19. A great deal of additional support for this hypothesis comes from Wills, *Inventing America*, pp. 176–180.

31. Conant, *Thomas Jefferson*, p. 19.

32. Ibid.

33. Ibid., p. 37.

34. Mead, *Lively Experiment*, p. 68.

35. In Koch and Peden, *Life and Writings*, pp. 632–634.

36. Cf. Heslep, *Thomas Jefferson*, p. 50.

37. Tyack, *Turning Points*, p. 85.

38. Ibid., p. 88.

39. Letter to John Adams, Aug. 15, 1820, in Koch and Peden, *Life and Writings*, p. 701. "In subsequent proposals for higher education Jefferson omitted theology. It was not science but fraud, a subject which cannot be justified educationally, which cannot be demonstrated to be a useful science, and which therefore has no place in any valid scheme of education" (Healey, *Jefferson*, p. 216).

40. Jefferson, "Report of the Commissioners Appointed to Fix the Site of the University of Virginia . . ." (The "Rockfish Gap Report"), in Honeywell, *Educational Work*, pp. 249–250.

41. Ibid., pp. 253–256. See also letter to John Adams, July 5, 1814; letter to George Ticknor, Nov. 25, 1817; minutes of the Board of Visitors of the University of Virginia, Mar. 4, 1825; all in Gordon Lee, ed., *Crusade Against Ignorance: Thomas Jefferson on Education* (New York: Teachers College, Columbia University, 1961), pp. 109ff.

42. Letter to William Short, Oct. 31, 1819, in Koch and Peden, *Life and Writings*, p. 694.

43. Letter to Thomas Cooper, Nov. 2, 1822, in Gordon Lee, ed., *Crusade Against Ignorance*, p. 79.

44. Healey, *Jefferson*, p. 177.

45. Tyack, *Turning Points*, p. 91. Cf. the recent treatment of Jefferson in Eva T. H. Braun, *Paradoxes of Education in a Republic* (Chicago: University of Chicago Press, 1979).

46. Healey, *Jefferson*, p. 218.

47. See Leonard Labaree et al., eds., *The Papers of Benjamin Franklin* (New Haven: Yale University Press, 1961), III, 399–421, and IV, 102–108.

48. The deistic foundations of Franklin's public religion are clearly

evident in his catalogue of moral virtues (*Autobiography*) and are well summarized in Tyack, *Turning Points,* p. 54.

49. See Cremin, *American Education,* pp. 260–264.

50. Reprinted in Frederick Rudolph, ed., *Essays on Education in the Early Republic* (Cambridge: Harvard University Press, 1965), pp. 3–23. This collection includes the plans for a national system of education proposed for the early days of the republic by Benjamin Rush, Noah Webster, Robert Coram, Simeon Dogget, Samuel Harrison Smith, Amable-Louis-Rose Du Courteil, and Samuel Knox. For a comprehensive account of the influence of French and English liberalism on the educational thought of the Revolutionary and post-Revolutionary generation of American intellectuals, see Allen O. Hansen, *Liberalism and American Education in the Eighteenth Century* (New York: Macmillan and Co., 1926).

51. Rush, in Rudolph, *Essays,* pp. 4–5.

52. Ibid., p. 5.

53. Ibid., p. 10. In 1791 Robert Coram of Wilmington, Delaware, articulated similar sentiments in an essay exploring the relation of political order and education. Coram argued that only a system of national education could ensure social integration. Without universal public education, Coram asked, "What is the bond of society, but a rope of sand, incapable of supporting its own weight? A heterogeneous jumble of contradications and absurdity, from which the subject knows not how to extricate himself" (Coram, "Political Inquiries: to Which is Added, a Plan for the General Establishment of Schools throughout the United States," in ibid., pp. 81–145).

54. According to Rush, "Such is my veneration for every religion that reveals the attributes of the Deity, or a future state of rewards and punishments, that I had rather see the opinions of Confucious or Mohammed inculcated upon our youth than see them grow up wholly devoid of a system of religious principles. But the religion I mean to recommend in this place is the religion of JESUS CHRIST" (ibid., p. 10).

55. Ibid., pp. 10–11.

56. Ibid., p. 14.

57. Ibid., p. 15.

58. Ibid., p. 9.

59. Ibid., p. 17.

60. Ibid., pp. 17–18.

61. Ibid., p. 16. The public school system in Rush's mind was to be a vehicle for the police power of the state. Indeed, one of the arguments he offers as to why it was proper to tax everyone for the support of the schools was that schools would be the most efficient way of controlling the unruly (ibid, pp. 6–7).

62. Noah Webster, "On Education of Youth in America" (1790), in ibid., p. 45.

63. Ibid. Once again it is evident that concern for virtue was a dominant theme in the educational plans of the early supporters of public education. For Webster "The *virtues* of men are of more consequence to society than their *abilities,* and for this reason the *heart* should be cultivated with more assiduity than the head" (ibid., p. 67).

64. Ibid., p. 72.

65. Ibid., p. 65.

66. Ibid., p. 64. Webster strongly believed in the need to nurture in Americans a nationalistic consciousness of their traditions and future

glory. His spelling books, especially the "blue-back speller" (A Grammatical Institute of the English Language: Part I), grammars, readers, and dictionaries were all designed to this end.

67. Hansen, *Liberalism*, p. 110.

68. Rudolph, *Essays*, p. 190.

69. Ibid., p. 190.

70. Cambacérès (1753–1824) played an important role in drafting the Napoleonic Civil Code. Under Napoleon the family came to be conceived as a mere instrument of the state.

71. Mead, *Lively Experiment*, pp. 66–67.

72. See Jerald C. Brauer, "The Rule of the Saints in American Politics," *Church History*, 27 (1958), 240–255; and J. F. Maclear, " 'The True American Union' of Church and State: The Reconstruction of the Theocratic Tradition," *Church History*, 28 (1959), 41–62.

CHAPTER 4

1. This point is made clear by Jefferson in his autobiography. See *Writings,* ed. Ford, I, 69.

2. In 1779 Jefferson introduced into the Virginia legislature a proposal designed to reform higher education in terms of his enlightenment perspective. "A Bill for Amending the Constitution of the College of William and Mary" called for a change in the original charter to allow for the expansion from six professors (two of whom were to teach theology) to eight professors (none of whom were to teach religion). Despite the failure of Jefferson's bill in the legislature, he was able to achieve the same goal some years later as a member of the board of visitors of William and Mary. In his *Notes on Virginia* Jefferson recounted with pride the fact that although the original efforts to change the college had failed, the same task was accomplished by changing the subjects taught by the six professors. Not until his "Bill for the Establishment of District Colleges and University" (1817), which eventually led to the founding of the University of Virginia, was Jefferson again able to structure an educational institution that reflected his world and life view.

3. There was some legal precedent for the principle of federal support for education in the congressional legislation which established the land ordinances of 1785 and 1787. But while the ordinances required a state entering the Union to set aside land for schools, the implementation was left in the hands of state and local authorities.

4. Bailyn, *Education*, p. 11. See also John S. Whitehead, *The Separation of College and State: Columbia, Dartmouth, Harvard, and Yale, 1776–1876* (New Haven: Yale University Press, 1973).

5. Massachusetts Constitution of 1780, Chap. V, Sec. II. Reprinted in Francis Newton Thorpe, ed., *Federal and State Constitutions,* 7 vols. (Washington, 1909), V, 467.

6. Theodore Sizer's study of the growth of academies in the United States reports that there were at least 6,000 such institutions by the middle of the nineteenth century. Theodore Sizer, *The Age of Academies* (New York: Columbia University, Teachers College Press, 1964).

7. Katz defines "corporate voluntarism" as the conduct of *single* institutions as individual corporations. This is one of the four alternative

patterns of public education that received support from state governments in the first half of the nineteenth century. Three other patterns analyzed by Katz which will be discussed shortly are "democratic localism," "incipient bureaucracy," and "paternalistic voluntarism." Katz has made a significant contribution to a better understanding of the history of American education by uncovering and analyzing these different organizational patterns of early nineteenth century public schools (Katz, *Class, Bureaucracy, and Schools,* p. 22).

8. Ibid., p. 23.

9. Ibid., pp. 15–22.

10. Ibid., p. 28. For other defects in democratic localism see pp. 15–22; 28–30.

11. Ibid., p. 28.

12. Quoted in Jonathan C. Messerli, "Localism and State Control in Horace Mann's Reform of the Common Schools," *American Quarterly,* 17 (1965), 111. For an overview of the pre–Civil War reform movement, see Alice Felt Tyler, *Freedom's Ferment* (New York: Harper and Row, 1944).

13. Tyack, *Turning Points,* p. 125.

14. Horace Mann to Frederick Packard, July 22, 1838, in Raymond B. Culver, *Horace Mann and Religion in Massachusetts Public Schools* (New Haven: Yale University, 1929), p. 267.

15. Tyack, *Turning Points,* p. 124.

16. *The Common School Journal,* Feb. 15, 1840, pp. 54–56, reprinted in Rush Welter, ed., *American Writings on Popular Education: The Nineteenth Century* (Indianapolis: Bobbs-Merrill, 1971), p. 78 (italics in the original). Two other comments of Mann to Henry Barnard, leader of the common school movement in Connecticut, indicate that not only the impulse and the language but the style was that of a secular evangelist. Writing of the strain during his opponents' attempt to abolish the board of education in 1840, Mann remarked that he found "consolation" in "laboring in a cause, which has my whole heart. . . . I know it is the greatest of earthly causes. It is a part of my religion that it must prevail." Or again, "When I took my circuit last year I mounted *on top of a horse,* and went Paul Prying all along the way, and diverging off to the right or left, wherever I scented any improvement. I believe that was substantially the way that Peter the Hermit got up the Crusades." Quoted in Katz, *Class, Bureaucracy, and Schools,* pp. 44–45.

17. Professor Tyack has made this point well: "Nervous about their own 'Americanism', natives grew alarmed about assimilating the newcomers. When the teachers of Cincinnati discussed the immigrant problem, Calvin Stowe and William McGuffey argued that public schools held out the best hope of turning foreign children into Americans. No random education would do; it must be uniform and systematic. Americans must define what it meant to be American and must find ways of inculcating patriotism in the young. In the textbooks of McGuffey and his contemporaries children would find the national pattern" (Tyack, *Turning Points,* pp. 123–124).

18. Quoted in Lawrence A. Cremin, *The Republic and the School* (New York: Teachers College, Columbia University, 1951), p. 53. Merle E. Curti has concluded that the urban schoolmen took sides with the privileged class partly because they needed support from that quarter in their campaign and partly because they shared the same values and biases.

See Merle E. Curti, *The Social Ideas of American Educators* (Totawa, New Jersey: Little-Field, Adams & Co., 1959) and Sidney L. Jackson, *America's Struggle for Free Schools: Social Tensions and Education in New England and New York, 1827–42* (New York: Russell and Russell, 1965).

19. Katz, *Class, Bureaucracy, and Schools*, p. 40.

20. For a detailed analysis of the political battles between supporters of district schools and the educational reformers see Michael B. Katz, *The Irony of Early School Reform: Educational Innovation in Mid-Nineteenth Century Massachusetts* (Boston: Beacon Press, 1968), especially Part I, "Reform by Imposition: Social Origins of Educational Controversy," pp. 19–112. For a discussion of the struggle at the turn of the twentieth century in other parts of the country, see David B. Tyack, "City Schools: Centralization of Control at the Turn of the Century," in Jerry Israel, ed., *Building the Organizational Society: Essays on Associational Activities in Modern America* (New York: The Free Press, 1972).

21. If the educational views of the urban schoolmen were not accepted willingly by the people, then, Katz points out, the people were to be forced to conform: "If everyone was taxed for school support, if this was justified by the necessity of schooling for the preservation of urban social order, if the beneficial impact of schooling required the regular and prolonged attendance of *all* children and finally, if persuasion and a variety of experiments had failed to bring all the children into the school — then, clearly, education had to be compulsory. In the crunch, social change would be imposed" (Katz, *Class, Bureaucracy, and Schools*, p. 48; italics in the original). In 1851 Massachusetts passed the first general compulsory education law and by 1890 twenty-seven state legislatures had passed similar laws. And yet, according to an 1889 survey, in all but a handful of cities and states like Massachusetts and Connecticut, the laws were not enforced. In several cases state superintendents of education did not even know there was such legislation. After 1890, however, compulsory schooling increased as states passed more effective laws. See Tyack, "Ways of Seeing: An Essay on the History of Compulsory Schooling," *Historical Educational Review*, 36 (1976), 361–362.

22. The use of schooling to inculate values and political order was a feature of both European liberalism (French educational writers after the 1789 revolution) and European conservatism (Prussia in the nineteenth century).

23. *Report of the Committee on Education of the House of Representatives*, Mar. 7, 1840, in Welter, *American Writings*, p. 91. Orestes Brownson also opposed the establishment of a centralized state school system. He warned his fellow Massachusetts citizens that "We may as well have a religion established by law as a system of education, and the government educate and appoint the pastors of our churches, as well as the instructors of our children" (in Katz, *Class, Bureaucracy, and Schools*, p. 18).

24. *Report of the Committee . . .* , p. 92. The House committee's argument also included the following: "That must, indeed, be an uninteresting course of reading, which would leave untouched either of these subjects [religion and politics]; and he must be a heartless writer, who can treat religious or political subjects, without affording any indication of his political or religious opinions. Books that confine themselves to the mere statement of undisputed propositions, whether in politics, religion, or morals, must be meagre indeed; nor is it possible to abstract, from treatises on these subjects, all that would give offence, without abstracting, at the same time, the whole substance of the matter. Mere abstract

propositions are of very little interest—it is their practical application to particular cases, in which all readers, and especially young readers, are principally interested. It is not sufficient, and it ought not to be, that a book contains nothing which we believe to be false. If it omit to state what we believe to be true; if it founds itself upon vague generalities, which will equally serve the purpose of all reasoners alike, this very omission to state what we believe to be the truth, becomes, in our eyes, a fault of the most serious character" (p. 92).

25. Katz, *Class, Bureaucracy, and Schools*, p. 39.

26. For an overview of the educational scene in New York City before the nineteenth century as well as a statistical accounting of the educational opportunities available between 1638 and 1782, see Cremin, *American Education*, pp. 534–541 and C. J. Mahoney, *The Relation of the State to Religious Education in Early New York, 1633–1825* (Washington, D.C.: Catholic University of America Press, 1941), chap. 1.

27. Diane Ravitch, *The Great School Wars, New York City, 1805–1973* (New York: Basic Books, 1974), p. 7.

28. Ibid.

29. By the legislative act passed on Mar. 12, 1813, the Commissioners of School Moneys were directed to pay the moneys received by them to "the trustees of the Free School Society in the city of New York and to the trustees of teachers of the Orphan Asylum Society, the Society of the Economical School in the city of New York, the African Free School, and of such incorporated religious societies in said city as now support, or hereafter shall establish, charity schools within the said city, who may apply for the same" (quoted in W. M. Oland Bourne, *History of the Public School Society of the City of New York* [New York: W. M. Wood and Co., 1870], p. 725).

30. The 1813 law stated that the "distribution shall be made to each school in proportion to the average number of children between the ages of four and sixteen years taught therein the year preceding such distribution, free of expense" (ibid., p. 68).

31. John Webb Pratt offers the following explanation for the development of New York City's subsidized, pluralized structure of education: "The explanation for this arrangement, seemingly contradicted by the policy of publicly managed schools enacted for upstate in 1812, was that the idea of public education did not yet include a clearcut distinction between 'public' and 'private' means of instruction. The state saw as its objective the encouragement of teaching in good citizenship. Schools as physical entities were but means to this end, requiring the public's serious attention only where such buildings were nonexistent, as was the case upstate but not in New York City. To a government of limited means, there were also obvious economies in such a policy" (John Webb Pratt, *Religion, Politics and Diversity: The Church-State Theme in New York History* [Ithaca, New York: Cornell University Press, 1967], pp. 165–166).

32. Katz, *Class, Bureaucracy, and Schools*, pp. 7–15.

33. "Act Passed by the Legislature of the State Relative to the Public School Society of New York, passed April 9, 1805" reprinted in *By-Laws of the Trustees of the Public School Society, of New York, As Revised and Adopted, January, 1833, and November, 1836*, Appendix, pp. 45–48. Katz refers to the structure of nineteenth-century public school education as "paternalistic voluntarism." The society was a private organization composed of upper-class philanthropists.

34. The "By-Laws" of the society stipulated that the "Mayor, Re-

corder, Aldermen and Assistants of the city of New York shall and may be *ex officio* members of said Corporation" (*By-Laws of the Trustees of the Public School Society*, p. 48).

35. Katz, *Class, Bureaucracy, and Schools*, p. 7.

36. Ibid. Until 1845 the society's schools were for boys only.

37. State legislature appropriated funds for the society's "peculiar privilege" by an act entitled "An Act to Log a duty on strong liquors, and for regulating inns and taverns" on Feb. 27, 1807. The act called for the appropriation of a "sum of four thousand dollars and every year thereafter for the purpose of exacting a suitable building or buildings for the instruction of poor children" (quoted in *By-Laws of the Trustees of the Public School Society*, p. 50).

38. Timothy L. Smith, "Protestant Schooling and American Nationality, 1800-1850," *The Journal of American History*, 53 (1967), 683.

39. For a perceptive analysis of this struggle and the recognition that, although the specific political contest was resolved, the underlying philosophical dispute remained only to break out again and again, consult Ravitch's *The Great School Wars, New York City, 1805–1973* and John Webb Pratt, *Religion, Politics and Diversity*.

40. Smith, "Protestant Schooling," pp. 685–686.

41. The society argued straightforwardly that having to share with the Baptists moneys from New York City's portion of the common school fund meant a reduction of funds to itself. What the society particularly feared was that other religious groups would follow the Baptist lead and further reduce its share of state funds. Since the Free School Society did not enjoy wide private financial support the trustees realized that without state support the society's schools could not survive. The trustees' position was published in the *Nineteenth Annual Report of the Trustees of the Free School Society of New York; With an Appendix*, 1824, pp. 17–18.

42. Quoted in Katz, *Class, Bureaucracy, and Schools*, p. 7.

43. Smith, "Protestant Schooling," p. 687.

44. Pratt, *Religion, Politics and Diversity*, p. 167. The full report of the legal committee is reprinted in Bourne, *History*, pp. 713–721.

45. The Baptists argued that "their program was as non-sectarian as the Free School Society, since they used the same curriculum, relied upon the same Lancastrian methods, and employed the same non-denominational catechism for religious instruction that had recently been in use in the Society's schools" (Smith, "Protestant Schooling," p. 687).

46. "An Act in relation to the Free-School Society of New York, passed January 28th, 1826," in Bourne, *History*, pp. 101–102. The society legally remained a private philanthropic organization run by a self-perpetuating board of trustees.

47. Ibid. To the argument that if the Baptist schools and other such institutions did not receive public funds they would cease to exist, the society responded: "Should the church school, however, be partially or wholly discontinued, your committee does not believe that any disadvantages to the public, or to the children attending them, will arise; as the means will be provided for educating them elsewhere, and probably in a more economical, and as well, if not in a superior manner" ("Report of a Committee of the Trustees of The Free-School Society On the Distribution of the Common School Fund," quoted in ibid., p. 89). During the next seven years the Baptist schools went out of existence (ibid., p. 124).

48. Smith, "Protestant Schooling," p. 687.

49. The standard work on immigration in this period is M. L. Hansen, *The Atlantic Migration, 1607–1860* (New York: Harper and Row, 1961).

50. Bourne, *History*, p. 124.

51. Ibid., p. 132.

52. Ibid., p. 134.

53. Ibid., p. 136 (italics added).

54. Ibid.

55. Portions of "manual" reprinted in ibid., pp. 642–644 (italics in original).

56. Bourne, *History*, p. 139.

57. Ibid.

58. For an analysis of the nativist movement see Ray Billington, *The Protestant Crusade, 1800–1860* (Gloucester, Mass.: Peter Smith, 1964).

59. The details of the political struggle in New York are discussed by Pratt, *Religion, Politics and Diversity,* especially chap. VII, "Church, State and Education."

60. For research which demonstrates Seward's true commitment to minority rights see Henry J. Browne, "Public Support of Catholic Education in New York, 1825–1842: Some New Aspects," *The Catholic Historical Review*, 39 (1953), and Vincent Lannie, *Public Money and Parochial Education: Bishop Hughes, Governor Seward, and the New York School Controversy* (Cleveland: Case Western Reserve University, 1968), pp. 1–28.

61. Quoted in Glyndon G. Van Deusen, "Seward and the School Question Reconsidered," *The Journal of American History*, 52 (1965), 313.

62. Ibid., p. 314. As to exactly what Seward had in mind with this proposal, Van Deusen points out that "It is clear enough what sort of teachers he wished for the children of foreigners, but he did not indicate whether he wished them to teach in public or parochial institutions. A few years later he told a friend that what he had in mind was 'to let the Catholics support schools of their own and receive their own share of the public monies', but this may have been hindsight" (ibid). John Webb Pratt's research supports Seward's contention that he "was suggesting that the state support sectarian schools, more specifically Catholic schools" (*Religion, Politics and Diversity*, p. 176).

63. For a discussion of the Catholic position before the arrival of Bishop Hughes, see Browne, "Public Support," pp. 1–11. John R. G. Hassard has written a biography of Bishop Hughes, *Life of the Most Reverend John Hughes* (New York: Appleton and Co., 1865).

64. Petition quotes from the Public School Society's 1827 Report. The entire petition is printed in Welter, *American Writings*, pp. 98–109.

65. Ibid., p. 104 (italics added).

66. Ibid., p. 105. Hughes formulated the dilemma in the following way: The Public School Society members "profess to exclude all sectarianism from their schools. If they do not exclude sectarianism, they are avowedly no more entitled to the school funds than your petitioners, or any other denomination of professing Christians. If they do, as they profess, exclude sectarianism, then your petitioners contend that they exclude Christianity; and leave to the advantage of infidelity the tendencies which are given to the minds of youth by the influence of this feature and pretension of their system" (ibid).

67. Hughes, "The Petition of the Catholics of the City of New York," Sept. 21, 1840, from *Documents of the Board of Aldermen of the City of*

New York, Vol. VII, No. 40 (1840–1841), reprinted in Welter, *American Writings,* p. 106.

68. Katz, *Class, Bureaucracy, and Schools,* p. 10.

69. Ibid. De Witt Clinton, president of the board, declared in 1809 that the Lancasterian system "is, in education, what the . . . machines for abridging labor and expense are in the mechanic arts." The system arrived "at its object with the least possible trouble and the least possible expense" (quoted in ibid.). For a fuller defense of the Lancasterian system by Clinton consult Wilson Smith's collection of documents entitled *Theories of Education in Early America, 1655–1819* (Indianapolis: Bobbs-Merrill, 1973).

70. Katz, *Class, Bureaucracy, and Schools,* p. 11.

71. Ibid.

72. For a discussion of the nonsectarian but essentially religious basis of Lancaster's program and its easy adaptability to the objectives of the New York Public School Society, see Timothy L. Smith, "Protestant Schooling," pp. 684–685.

73. Pratt, *Religion, Politics and Diversity,* p. 178.

74. Ibid., p. 179. For an important theoretical defense made in 1841 by the New York secretary of state, John C. Spencer, in support of the Catholic claim that justice demanded a proportional share of public funds for their schools, see Rockne McCarthy et al., *Society, State, and Schools: A Case for Structural and Confessional Pluralism* (Grand Rapids: Eerdmans, 1980), pp. 90–92.

75. For a discussion of the direct Catholic venture into politics (the Catholic ticket of 1841) see ibid., pp. 183–186.

76. Ibid., p. 183.

77. Quoted in ibid., p. 187. The Massachusetts school struggle culminated in a similar law. A constitutional amendment of 1855 stated: "All moneys raised by taxation in the towns and cities for the support of public schools, all moneys which may be appropriated by the state for the support of common schools, shall be applied to, and expended in, no other schools than those which are conducted according to law, under the order and superintendence of the authorities of the town or city in which the money is to be expended; and such moneys shall never be appropriated to any religious sect for the maintenance, exclusively, of its own school" (eighteenth amendment to the Massachusetts constitution, adopted 1855; see Thorpe, *Federal and State Constitutions,* p. 1918).

78. Lannie, *Public Money,* p. x.

79. Quoted in ibid.

80. Ibid.

81. Ibid., p. xi.

82. Ibid., p. 193. Lawrence Cremin discusses this historiographical tradition in *The Wonderful World of Ellwood Patterson Cubberly* (New York: Teachers College Press, 1965).

83. Timothy L. Smith, "Protestant Schooling"; David Tyack, "The Kingdom of God and the Common School: Protestant Ministers and the Educational Awakening in the West," *Harvard Educational Review,* 36 (1966), 447–469; Robert Michaelsen, *Piety in the Public Schools: Trends and Issues in the Relationship Between Religion and the Public School in the U.S.* (New York: Macmillan, 1970); Donald Pitzer, "Christianity in the Public Schools," in Robert G. Clouse, Robert D. Linder, and Richard V. Pierard, eds., *Protest and Politics* (Greenwood, South Carolina: The

Attic Press, Inc., 1968), pp. 151–181.

84. Presbyterian and Congregational ministers representing New England missionary societies or the American Home Mission Society combined with Baptist and Methodist preachers to guarantee that frontiersmen did not escape Christian civilization by falling victim to Romanism, barbarism and skepticism.

85. Before the American Revolution, in New York, Maryland, and South Carolina the traditional pattern of the establishment of a "single" church had evolved toward a "multiple" form of Christian establishment. See Cushing Strout, *New Heavens*, pp. 83–84, and R. Freeman Butts, *The American Tradition in Religion and Education* (Boston: Beacon Press, 1950).

86. Wisconsin (1848), Art. 1, sec. 18, pp. 4078–4079; Michigan (1850), Art. 4, sec. 40, p. 1950; Indiana (1851), Art. 1, sec. 6, p. 1074; Oregon (1857), Art. 1, sec. 5, p. 2998; and Minnesota (1857), Art. 1, sec. 16.

87. Quoted in R. Freeman Butts, *The American Tradition*. Grant urged there be a complete and absolute separation between church and state. This included doing away with tax exemptions for church property.

88. Ibid., p. 143.

89. Illinois ex rel. McCollum v. Board of Education, 333 U.S. 203 (1948), p. 469.

90. Ibid., p. 470. State constitutional provisions related to the funding of schools are many and varied. See James R. Brown, "State Constitutions and Religion in Education," in Daniel D. McGarry and Leo Ward, eds., *Educational Freedom and the Case for Government Aid to Students in Independent Schools* (Milwaukee: Bruce Publishing Co., 1966), pp. 163–183.

CHAPTER 5

1. See especially Hamilton v. Regents of University of California, 293 U.S. 245 (1934); Cantwell v. Connecticut, 310 U.S. 296 (1940); and Everson v. Board of Education, 310 U.S. 1 (1947). Henry J. Abraham, *Freedom and the Court*, 3rd ed. (New York: Oxford University Press, 1977), pp. 249–251.

2. Thompson, "Reasoning, Religion and the Court," in *Public Policy* (Cambridge, Mass.: Harvard University Press, 1967), pp. 360–362.

3. *Abington School District* v. *Schempp* and Murray v. Curlett, 374 U.S. 203 (1963); Engel v. Vitale, 370 U.S. 421 (1962); Everson v. Board of Education of Ewing Township, N.J., 330 U.S. 1 (1947); Illinois ex rel. McCollum v. Board of Education, 333 U.S. 203 (1948).

4. Thompson, "Reasoning," p. 367. Along these lines, Harold Stahmer asks the rhetorical question: "Is the purpose of Constitutional adjudication, for example, that of preserving an eighteenth-century principle of religious and political liberty based on a religious outlook that is being challenged in some quarters and regarded as obsolete in still others?" "Defining Religion: Federal Aid and Academic Freedom," in Donald A. Giannella, ed., *Religion and the Public Order* (Chicago: University of Chicago Press, 1964), p. 123.

5. Howe, *The Garden and the Wilderness*, p. 146.

6. Mead, *Lively Experiment*, p. 135.

7. Smith, *Religious Liberty*, pp. 120–121.

8. Arons, "The Separation of School and State: *Pierce* Reconsidered," *Harvard Educational Review*, 46 (1976), 97.

9. Ibid., p. 77.

10. See, for example, Anson Phelps Stokes and Leo Pfeffer, *Church and State in the United States*, revised one-volume edition (New York: Harper and Row, 1964). Note the discussion in Thompson, "Reasoning," pp. 378ff.; and in William A. Carroll, "The Constitution, The Supreme Court, and Religion," *American Political Science Review*, 51 (1967), 658ff.

11. See Black's argument, *Everson*, 15ff.

12. The "child benefit" principle was established in 1930 by the Court's decision in *Cochran* v. *Louisiana State Board of Education*, 281 U.S. 370, when it determined that government funds for "secular" textbooks for parochial school students is a legitimate expense supporting the "public purpose" by benefiting the child alone while not being a direct subsidy to religious schools.

13. See Justice Douglas's arguments along this line in *Schempp* and also in *Lemon et al.* v. *Kurtzman*, 403 U.S. at 641. Also note E. A. Smith, *Religious Liberty*, pp. 261–262.

14. Thompson, "Reasoning," p. 379; E. A. Smith, *Religious Liberty*, p. 306. For important critical discussions of *Everson* and *McCollum* see Carroll, pp. 658ff.; and John Courtney Murray, "Law or Prepossessions?" in Robert G. McCloskey, ed., *Essays in Constituional Law* (New York: Vintage Books, 1957), pp. 316–347.

15. Wilbur G. Katz, "Freedom of Religion and State Neutrality," *University of Chicago Law Review*, 20 (1952–53), 428. Cf. Abraham, *Freedom*, pp. 309ff.

16. Thompson's summary of different kinds of "neutrality" arguments includes (1) the Jeffersonian idea of a "common" general core of religious/moral truth which we analyzed in Chapter Two; (2) the idea that the state could be neutral with respect to religion if it distributed its aid "non-preferentially"; and (3) an argument made by Philip Kurland in his *Religion and the Law* (Chicago: Aldine, 1962), which stresses that "the religion clauses should be read to mean that 'the government cannot utilize religion as a standard for action or inaction because these clauses prohibit classification in terms of religion either to confer a benefit or to impose a burden' " (Thompson "Reasoning," p. 386). It will become clear as our argument develops that while we reject all of Thompson's categories, there are elements of (2) and (3) which can be understood more adequately from another point of view. See also Nicholas Wolterstorff, "Neutrality and Impartiality," in Theodore Sizer, ed., *Religion and Public Education* (Boston: Houghton Mifflin, 1967), pp. 3–21.

17. Thompson, "Reasoning," p. 387. Wolterstorff works with much the same standard as acceptable: "Nothing that the public school says or does shall have as its purpose, or as an avoidable feature or effect of its manner of achieving its purpose, the manifesting of approval or disapproval of any citizen's religion or irreligion" (Wolterstorff, "Neutrality," p. 16).

18. Thompson, "Reasoning," pp. 388–389.

19. *Schempp*, p. 226 (italics in original).

20. *Schempp*, p. 313.

21. *Lemon I*, pp. 612, 613.

22. Ibid., p. 614.

23. Ibid., pp. 616–617.

24. Justices Douglas, Stewart, and Brennan all raise objections in this connection. Douglas says, for example, that "the school is an organism living on one budget. What the taxpayers give for salaries of those who teach only the humanities or science without any trace of proselytizing enables the school to use all of its own funds for religious training" (ibid., p. 641). See Brennan's comments at 657.

25. Ibid., pp. 622–623.

26. Ibid., p. 625.

27. Ibid., p. 630.

28. *Yoder*, p. 215.

29. Ibid., pp. 215–216.

30. Quoted in *Yoder*, p. 248. See also Torcaso v. Watkins, 367 U.S. 488 (1961).

31. 421 U.S. 349 (1975).

32. Rehnquist's opinion in *Meek*, p. 395.

33. Respectively: 426 U.S. 736; 433 U.S. 229; and 63 L Ed 2d 94.

34. Blackmun, *Roemer*, p. 754.

35. Blackmun, *Wolman*, p. 255.

36. Powell, *Wolman*, pp. 262–264.

37. Stevens, *Wolman*, pp. 265–266.

CHAPTER 6

1. Harold Stahmer comments, with regard to the strict separationists, that "the principle of 'neutrality' with respect to church-state questions espoused among religious supporters of a strict separatist position, is as strong an ideological position and bias as that found among religious opponents of this position" ("Defining Religion," p. 119).

2. "The effect of the *Torcaso* decision [Torcaso v. Watkins, 367 U.S. 488 (1961)]," according to Stahmer, "was to give the broadest possible interpretation to the term [*religion*], since the Court held that disbelief as well as belief were protected by the First Amendment. The Court's position was that '. . . neither a State nor the Federal Government can constitutionally force a person "to profess a belief or disbelief in any religion." Neither can constitutionally pass laws nor impose requirements which aid all religions as against non-believers, and neither can aid those religions based on belief in the existence of God as against those religions founded on different beliefs' [*Torcaso*, 495].

"The effect of the *Torcaso* decision is to extend protection not only to religions such as Taoism which do not believe in the existence of God in the Western sense, but also to groups such as Ethical Culture, many of whose members are atheists and agnostics, and to the *individual* atheist or non-believer" (ibid., pp. 131–132).

3. This is why Alexander Meikeljohn would argue that "The freedom of religion has the same basic justification as has the freedom of speech or of the press. In both sets of cases, a strong and passionate private desire is involved. But far deeper than this is public necessity. When men are trying to be self-governing, no other single factor of their

experience is more important to them than the freedom of their religion or of their nonreligion. The interpreting of our spiritual beliefs is a public enterprise of the highest order" (quoted in Carroll, "The Constitution," p. 671, from Meikeljohn's "Educational Cooperation Between Church and State," *Law and Contemporary Problems,* 14 [1949], 67).

4. Arons points out that one implication of the *Yoder* decision is that "any conflict between public schooling and a family's basic and sincerely held values interferes with the family's First Amendment rights. Thus, even though the opinion was couched in terms of religious beliefs and practices, the Chief Justice's recognition of the various elements of value inculcation, none of which is itself of religious character, has the effect of eroding the meaningfulness of the distinction between secular and religious values upon which the Court has relied so heavily" ("Separation of School and State," pp. 84–85).

5. In this regard we are arguing that an adequate constitutional recognition of religion must go hand in hand with an adequate constitutional recognition of the nature of persons, groups, institutions, and communities which happen to be religious. Thus, though we agree with Carroll's comments that follow, we recognize the necessity of a prior step. Carroll argues that the neutrality required by the establishment clause of the First Amendment "must be exercised not merely in regard to various sects, but across the whole range of belief and disbelief. The failure of the Court to employ the concept of neutrality, instead of its untenable *Everson* definition, may have arisen from its failure to conceive of neutrality as extending to all forms of religious belief and nonbelief. This failure may, in turn, have arisen from a failure to define religion for constitutional purposes.

"In any case, if the concept of government neutrality is to be meaningful, it is necessary to define religion for constitutional purposes, particularly in relation to the establishment clause. It is a commonplace to say that the free exercise clause applies to nonbelievers as well as believers. What has not been as clearly recognized, and what cannot be applied until there is a definition of the constitutional meaning of religion, is the concept that the establishment clause must also logically apply to nonbelief as well as to belief. Without such a recognition neutrality will be impossible, for either the government will give its aid impartially to those organizations meeting the traditional theistic concept of religion, ignoring those outside that concept . . . , or it will deny all aid to traditional religion, with consequent advantage to nonbelievers" (Carroll, "The Constitution," pp. 663–664).

6. For discussion of *Reynolds* see E. A. Smith, *Religious Liberty,* pp. 255ff.; Stahmer, "Defining Religion," p. 133; and J. Morris Clark, "Guidelines for the Free Exercise Clause," *Harvard Law Review,* 83 (1969–70), 327ff.

7. Smith, *Religious Liberty,* p. 263.

8. Ibid., pp. 256–257.

9. *Sherbert,* p. 404, as quoted in Abraham, *Freedom,* p. 288 (italics in the original).

10. E. A. Smith, *Religious Liberty,* p. 320.

11. *Yoder,* p. 220.

12. As Professor Kurland says, "The action-belief dichotomy is obviously inadequate to attainment of the stated goals of the religion clauses" (*Religion and the Law,* p. 111).

13. For a discussion of the way that Justice Frankfurter was posing

these questions (within the framework of the religious/secular dualism) in the early 1940s, see E. A. Smith, *Religious Liberty*, pp. 265– 266.

14. This is Carroll's point, "The Constitution," p. 663.

15. Especially clear in *Sherbert;* see Abraham, *Freedom*, p. 288, and E. A. Smith, *Religious Liberty*, p. 320.

16. For a helpful discussion of the identity and rights of institutions, see chapter 3 of McCarthy et al., *Society, State, and Schools*, pp. 51– 78.

17. E. A. Smith asks, "But who is to determine the religious or secular character of social ethics? For the state to declare all social ethics secular is virtually a doctrine of religion in itself" *(Religious Liberty*, p. 357).

18. In a number of cases, from *Pierce* to the present, the Supreme Court has acknowledged the important right that parents, for example, have to decide about the education of their children — a right that may not be abridged by the government. In *Yoder* Chief Justice Burger stated: "We can accept it as settled, therefore, that, however strong the State's interest in universal compulsory education, it is by no means absolute to the exclusion or subordination of all other interests" (215). In the case of *Meyer* v. *Nebraska* (262 U.S. 390) in 1923, two years before *Pierce*, the Court upheld the right of a teacher to teach in German instead of English in a German-speaking community. In doing so the Court appealed to the prior rights of the individual over against the legitimate desire of a legislature to foster a "homogeneous people with American ideals. . . ." It "warned that homogeneity is not to be attained at the sacrifice of basic teacher, parental and child rights" (National Catholic Welfare Conference, "The Constitutionality of the Inclusion of Church-Related Schools in Federal Aid to Education," *Georgetown Law Journal*, 5 [1961]), 427– 428.

19. *Yoder*, pp. 210– 211.

20. Ibid., p. 217.

21. Ibid., p. 218.

22. Ibid., p. 213.

23. Burger in *Meek* (slip), p. 3.

24. Arons, "Separation of School and State," p. 78.

25. Quoted in ibid., p. 100.

26. Ibid., p. 100.

27. Ibid., p. 99.

28. See *Pierce*, pp. 534– 535; *Yoder*, pp. 213, 232; Arons, "Separation of School and State," p. 78.

29. The Ninth Amendment to the Constitution reads: "The enumeration in the Constitution, of certain rights, shall not be construed to deny or disparage others retained by the people." This seems to leave open the possiblity of there being other rights and obligations than those enumerated for individuals and for the federal government and the states. But it does not go on to identify or enumerate groups, institutions, or communities that might have such rights.

CHAPTER 7

1. This problem and possible solutions are discussed with great clarity in Kenneth Dolbeare, *Political Change in the United States: A Framework for Analysis* (New York: McGraw-Hill, 1974), passim.

2. Gabriel A. Almond, "Comparative Political Studies," *Journal of Politics,* 18 (1956), 391– 409.

3. Hans Daalder, "The Consociational Democracy Theme," *World Politics* 26 (1974), 606– 607. Daalder showed some amusement at the parochialism embodied in such conclusions.

4. Seymour Martin Lipset, *Political Man* (Garden City, New York: Anchor Books, 1963), especially pp. 70– 82.

5. Benjamin R. Barber, *The Death of Communal Liberty* (Princeton: Princeton University Press, 1974), p. 3.

6. Arend Lijphart, "Consociational Democracy," *World Politics* 21 (1969), passim.

7. Jurg Steiner, *Amicable Agreement Versus Majority Rule* (Chapel Hill: University of North Carolina Press, 1974), p. 5.

8. The definitive exploration of the topic, with references to all major works is Arend Lijphart, *Democracy in Plural Societies* (New Haven: Yale University Press, 1977), passim.

9. See the descriptions in Kurt Shell, *The Transformation of Austrian Socialism* (New York: State University of New York, 1962), pp. 35– 125; Johan Goudsblom, *Dutch Society* (New York: Random House, 1967), pp. 120– 127; J. P. Kruijt, "The Netherlands: The Influence of Denominationalism on Social Life and Organizational Patterns," in Kenneth McRae, ed., *Consociational Democracy* (Toronto: McClelland and Stewart Ltd., 1974), pp. 128– 136; Val Lorwin, "Belgium: Conflict and Compromise," in McRae, *Consociational,* pp. 179– 206; Hans Daalder, "On Building Consociational Nations: The Cases of the Netherlands and Switzerland," in *Consociational,* pp. 107– 124.

10. The segmentation of consociational societies along religious, linguistic, or ideological lines is neither uniform nor static. Observers who have pointed out the recent decline in group life include Martine de Ridder, "Images of Belgian Politics: The Effects of Cleavages on the Political System," *Legislative Studies Quarterly,* 3 (1978), 92; Arend Lijphart, "The Netherlands: Continuity and Change in Voting Behavior," in Richard Rose, ed., *Electoral Behavior* (New York: Free Press, 1974), p. 229; William T. Bluhm, *Building an Austrian Nation* (New Haven: Yale University Press, 1973), pp. 114– 128; Earl H. Fry and Gregory A. Raymond, *The Other Western Europe* (Santa Barbara: ABC-Clio, 1980), pp. 132– 135. The leading causes seem to be a decline in religious/ideological conviction and a cosmopolitanism deriving from higher levels of communication, transportation, and economic modernization. At the same time, a resurgence of ethnic identity has occured all over Europe. See Walker Connor, "The Political Significance of Ethnonationalism Within Western Europe," in Abul Said and Luiz R. Simmons, eds., *Ethnicity in an International Context* (New Brunswick, N.J.: Transaction Books, 1976), pp. 110– 133; Milton J. Esman, ed., *Ethnic Conflict in the Western World* (Ithaca: Cornell University Press, 1977), passim. In the Netherlands a small conservative Calvinist group has actually created a new pillar which includes a political party, newspaper, school system, and radio and television capacities. In general, however, the older forms of group life seem to be on the wane, though they demonstrate remarkable staying power as pointed out by Rodney P. Stiefbold, "Segmented Pluralism and Consociational Democracy in Austria," in Martin O. Heisler, ed., *Politics in Europe* (New York: David McKay Co., 1974), p. 141.

11. Philip J. Idenburg, "Financial Equalization in the Nether-

lands," in Robert J. Havighurst, ed., *Comparative Perspectives on Education* (Boston: Little, Brown and Co., 1968), p. 271 (italics added).

12. Hyman G. Rickover, *Swiss Schools and Ours* (Boston: Little, Brown and Co., 1962), p. 42.

13. David O. Moberg, "Religion and Society in the Netherlands and America," *American Quarterly*, 13 (1961), 16.

14. Martin O. Heisler, "Institutionalizing Social Cleavages in a Cooptive Polity: The Growing Importance of the Output Side in Belgium," in Martin O. Heisler, ed., *Politics in Europe* (New York: David McKay Co., 1974), p. 218.

15. Hans Daalder and Galen Irwin, "Interests and Institutions in the Netherlands: An Assessment by the People and by Parliament," *The Annals* (May 1974), p. 59; A. Stafford Clayton, *Religion and Schooling* (Waltham, Mass.: Blaisdell Publishing Co., 1969), p. 123.

16. See, for example, the note in Bernard Zylstra, *From Pluralism To Collectivism* (Assen, the Netherlands: Van Gorcum and Co., 1970), p. 14; R. E. M. Irving, *Christian Democracy in France* (London: Allen and Unwin, 1973), pp. 60–61.

17. Daalder, "Consociational Theme," p. 617.

18. Shell, *Austrian Socialism,* p. 90.

19. For descriptions and discussions of proportionality and non-majoritarianism see Gerhard Lembruch, "A Non-Competitive Pattern of Conflict Management in Liberal Democracies: The Case of Switzerland, Austria and Lebanon," in McRae, *Consociational,* passim; Jurg Steiner, "The Principles of Majority and Proportionality," in McRae, *Consociational,* passim; Steiner, *Amicable Agreement,* passim; Lijphart, *Democracy,* pp. 25–41; James A. Dunn, Jr., "Consociational Democracy and Language Conflict," *Comparative Political Studies,* 5 (1972), 17.

20. For a discussion of the language regions and cultural councils see James A. Dunn, Jr., "The Constitutional Protection of Minorities in Belgium," *Politics 73,* March 1973, pp. 1–6, 9–18.

21. Kurt Steiner, *Politics in Austria* (Boston: Little, Brown and Co., 1972), pp. 88–90, 390–397.

22. Lembruch, "Non-Competitive Pattern," p. 95.

23. J. Steiner, "Majority and Proportionality," p. 103.

24. Bluhm, *Building An Austrian Nation,* p. 65.

25. Dunn, "Constitutional Protection," pp. 6–9, 11.

26. John Courtney Murray, "Law or Prepossessions?" in Robert McCloskey, ed., *Essays in Constitutional Law* (New York: Vintage Books, 1957), p. 334.

27. Michael Katz also calls attention to the need for political change before educational changes can take place in *Class, Bureaucracy, and Schools,* pp. 119–120.

28. Shell, *Austrian Socialism,* p. 185.

29. Ibid.

30. Benigno Benabarre, *Public Funds for Private Schools in a Democracy* (Manilla: M.C.S. Enterprises, 1958), p. 222.

31. K. Steiner, *Politics in Austria,* p. 203.

32. Ibid.

33. Eugene Egger and Emile Blanc, *Education in Switzerland* (Geneva: Swiss Educational Documentation Centre, July 1974), p. 3.

34. F. William O'Brien, "The Engel Case From a Swiss Perspective," *Michigan Law Review,* 61 (1963), 1069–1086.

35. Ibid., p. 1075.

36. Vernon Van Dyke, "Equality and Discrimination in Education: A Comparative and International Analysis," *International Studies Quarterly,* 17 (1973), 395.

37. Rickover, *Swiss Schools,* p. 42.

38. For an account see Keith Hill, "Belgium: Political Change in a Segmented Society," in Richard Rose, ed., *Electoral Behavior* (New York: Free Press, 1974), pp. 36–37.

39. Vernon Mallinson and Silvain DeCoster, "Church and State Education in Belgium," *Comparative Education Review,* 4 (1960), 46.

40. *Education in Belgium* (Brussels: Belgian Information and Documentation Institute, 1967), p. 4.

41. George Z. F. Bereday and Joseph Lauwerys, *Church and State in Education: The World Yearbook of Education, 1966* (New York: Harcourt, Brace and World, 1966), p. 335; Mallinson, "Church and State," p. 46.

42. Van Dyke, "Equality and Discrimination," pp. 391–392.

43. R. L. Planche, "Belgium," in L. Deighton, ed., *The Encyclopedia of Education,* I (New York: Macmillan, 1971), 451; Mallinson, "Church and State," p. 44. For more on Belgium, see J. Billiet, "Secularization and Compartmentalization in the Belgian Educational System," *Social Compass,* 20 (1973), 569–591.

44. The section draws on the account in Bereday, *Church and State in Education,* pp. 79–82.

45. Bereday, *Church and State in Education,* p. 82.

46. *The Kingdom of the Netherlands* (The Hague: Educational Ministry of Foreign Affairs, Government Printing Office, 1971), p. 31.

47. For a description see Edwin H. Palmer, "Freedom and Equity in Dutch Education," in Daniel McGarry and Leo Ward, eds., *Educational Freedom and the Case for Government Aid to Students in Independent Schools* (Milwaukee: Bruce Publishing Co., 1966), pp. 75–77.

48. Theodore Reller, "Public Funds for Religious Education: Canada, England and the Netherlands," in Donald Giannella, ed., *Religion and the Public Order: 1963* (Chicago: University of Chicago Press, 1964), p. 188.

49. Clayton, *Religion and Schooling,* p. 110.

50. Reller, "Public Funds," p. 187.

51. *The Kingdom of the Netherlands,* p. 32.

52. Ibid. (italics added).

53. Section 27 (3), final authorized text of 1948. A similar statement can be found in the United Nations' Declaration of the Rights of a Child, Principle VII, 1959.

54. Article II of the Additional Protocol, 1952.

55. See, for example, Benabarre, *Public Funds,* passim; McGarry and Ward, eds., *Educational Freedom,* especially chaps. IV, VI; A. C. F. Beales, "Church and State in Education," in Paul Nash, ed., *History and Education* (New York: Random House, 1970), pp. 256–282; Van Dyke, "Equality and Discrimination," pp. 375–404.

56. A common argument is that educational pluralism might be possible for small consociational states, but that in *large* countries with *many* religious communities like the United States the concept is simply unworkable. The experience of Canada is evidence that this is not necessarily the case. For a description of the pluralistic educational system in

many of the Canadian provinces see McCarthy et al., *Society, State, and Schools*, pp. 136–139.

CHAPTER 8

1. Many of the theoretical, political, and educational arguments in support of vouchers have been supplied by John Coons and Stephen Sugarman in *Education By Choice: The Case for Family Control* (Berkeley: University of California Press, 1978).

2. Arons, "Separation of School and State," p. 99.

3. For more on the pluralistic conception of society and the state which lies behind this paragraph and the arguments of the book as a whole, see McCarthy et al., *Society, State, and Schools*; James Skillen, ed., *Confessing Christ and Doing Politics* (Washington, D.C.: APJ Education Fund, 1982); Skillen, "The Development of Calvinistic Political Theory in the Netherlands" (diss., Duke University, 1974); Herman Dooyeweerd, *The Christian Idea of the State* (Nutley, N.J.: The Craig Press, 1968); Jan Dengerink, "A Christian Concept of Human Society," *The Gordon Review*, 6 (1961), 82–91; Bob Goudzwaard, *A Christian Political Option* (Toronto: Wedge Publishing Foundation, 1972); Rockne McCarthy, "American Civil Religion," in Skillen, ed., *Confessing Christ and Doing Politics*; H. Evan Runner, *Scriptural Religion and Political Task* (Toronto: Wedge Publishing Foundation, 1974); H. Van Riesen, *The Society of the Future* (Philadelphia: Presbyterian and Reformed Publishers, 1957); S. U. Zuidema, *Communication and Confrontation: A Philosophical Appraisal and Critique of Modern Society and Contemporary Thought* (Toronto: Wedge Publishing Foundation, 1972); Bernard Zylstra, *From Pluralism to Collectivism: The Development of Harold Laski's Political Thought* (New York: Humanities Press, 1970); Zylstra, "The Bible, Justice, and the State," in Skillen, ed., *Confessing Christ and Doing Politics*; L. Kalsbeek, *Contours of a Christian Philosophy* (Toronto: Wedge Publishing Foundation, 1975).

4. For more on this problem, see John A. Olthuis, *A Place to Stand: A Case for Support for All Public Schools* (Sarnia: The Ontario Alliance of Christian Schools, n.d.); Robert Carvill, "Unmasking Polite Totalitarianism," *Vanguard* (September 1971), pp. 7–11; Edwin H. Palmer, "Freedom and Equality in Dutch Education," in McGarry and Ward, eds., *Educational Freedom*, pp. 65–84; Calvin Seerveld, "The Christian School in American Democracy," in *Convention Addresses: 44th Annual Christian School Convention* (Grand Rapids: National Union of Christian Schools, 1964), pp. 2–19.

5. Rothbard, "Historical Origins," in William F. Rickenbacker, ed., *The Twelve Year Sentence: Radical Views of Compulsory Schooling* (New York: Dell, 1974), pp. 21–22. See also Rothbard's *Education, Free and Compulsory* (Menlo Park, Calif.: Center for Independent Education, 1972) and his "Total Reform: Nothing Less," in E. G. West, ed., *Nonpublic School Aid* (Lexington, Mass.: Lexington Books, 1976), pp. 102–107.

6. Spring, "Sociological and Political Ruminations," in Rickenbacker, *Twelve Year Sentence*, p. 155.

7. Ibid., p. 154.

8. See the several essays in Robert Carvill, ed., *To Prod the "Slumbering Giant": A Christian Approach to the Crisis in the Classroom* (Toronto: Wedge Publishing Foundation, 1972).

9. *Schooling in Capitalist America* (New York: Basic Books and Harper Colophon Books, 1976).

10. Ibid., p. 265.

11. Ibid., pp. 265–266.

12. Ibid., pp. 283–284.

13. Butts, "Assaults on a Great Idea," *The Nation,* Apr. 30, 1973, pp. 553–560.

14. Butts, "Public Education and Political Community," *History of Education Quarterly*, 14 (1974), 177.

15. Ibid.

16. Butts's perspective is premised upon an Enlightenment philosophy which treats *peoples* and social *structures* as if they were parts of a universal, moral, political community, rather than treating them as having their own identity and their own distinct tasks and responsibilities. In Butts's view this political community transcends and assumes unto itself all peoples. He is quite clear on this point: "In the United States the political community is symbolized in the term 'We the People' who represent the ultimate authority in the political system. What makes a diverse people into a 'we' are the common moral commitments and the shared sense of distinctive identity and cohesion that are essential for building, maintaining, and improving the basic political structure as well as the day-to-day processes of government decision-making" (ibid., p. 178). The essential purpose of public education is to establish and maintain this moral community. Schools (other institutions as well) along with peoples are simply *parts* of the universal *whole*.

17. "The original idea of American public education drew upon the Western stock of Enlightenment ideas which assumed that public education had primarily a political purpose in the modernization process" (ibid).

18. Ibid., p. 177.

19. The older studies of civic education by such prominent political scientists as Charles E. Merriam provide important insights into how education is often used for political purposes. Charles Edward Merriam, *The Making of Citizens: A Comparative Study of Methods of Civic Training* (Chicago: University of Chicago Press, 1931) and *Civic Education in America* (New York: Charles Scribner's and Sons, 1934). A series of studies was made of civic education in the late 1920s. The series included studies of Italy, Russia, Germany, England, France, Switzerland, Austria-Hungary, and the United States. Merriam's *The Making of Citizens* contains bibliographical citations for all the different studies. More recent studies of civic education include George Z. F. Bereday and Bonnie B. Stretch, "Political Education in the U. S. A. and the U. S. S. R.," *Comparative Education Review*, 7 (1963); Robert H. Wiebe, "The Social Functions of Public Education," *American Quarterly*, 21 (1969); R. Farnen, A. N. Oppenheim, and Judith Torney, *Civic Education in Ten Countries: An Empirical Study* (Stockholm, 1975); Rush Welter, "The Social Functions of Education," in J. R. Pole, ed., *The Advance of Democracy* (New York: Harper and Row, 1967); Charles R. Foster, "Civic Education in the United States and the Federal Republic of Germany," *International Journal of Political Education*, 1 (1977).

20. See Butts, *The American Tradition in Religion and Education*,

and "The Public Purpose of the Public School," *Teachers College Record*, 75 (1973).

21. For an analysis of the different kinds of political efforts that will be required, see chapter 7 ("Strategies for Constructive Change Toward Pluralism") in McCarthy et al., *Society, State, and Schools*.

22. See the testimony by Rockne McCarthy before the Senate Finance Committee in support of tuition tax relief bills (Hearings Before The Subcommittee on Taxation and Debt Management Generally of the Committee on Finance, United States Senate, Ninety-Fifth Congress, January 20, 1978 [Washington D.C.: U. S. Government Printing Office, 1978], pp. 499–504), and the testimony of James Skillen before the House Ways and Means Committee in support of tax credits for tuition expenses (Hearings Before the Committee on Ways and Means, House of Representatives, Ninety-Fifth Congress, February 16, 1978 [Washington, D.C.: U. S. Government Printing Office, 1978], pp. 391–396, 414–415.)